Writing Engagement
Involving Students in the Writing Process:
Grade 4

BY

JANET P. SITTER, Ph.D.

COPYRIGHT © 2002 Mark Twain Media, Inc.

ISBN 1-58037-197-3

Printing No. CD-1543

Mark Twain Media, Inc., Publishers
Distributed by Carson-Dellosa Publishing Company, Inc.

Table of Contents

Introduction

This book is a writing engagement resource for both teachers and students. Through these exercises, students will improve both their writing and their language skills. By evaluating their writing using the rubrics in the back of the book, students will sharpen their understanding of the writing process and their writing skills. Teachers will have a consistent process for teaching and evaluating student writing using the assessment rubrics provided.

There are five important features emphasized in this book: (1) the practice and apply student work pages; (2) the teacher evaluation rubrics; (3) the student writing rubrics; (4) the student writing prompts; and (5) the writing skills tests.

The Writing Process

1. **Prewriting:** Choose a topic; gather and organize ideas; identify the audience for the writing; identify the purpose of the writing; choose the appropriate format for the writing.

2. **Drafting:** Write a rough draft to get down the ideas; write beginnings that "grab" the reader's attention; emphasize ideas rather than mechanics.

3. **Revising:** Share writing with the group or teacher; reflect on comments and make substantive changes; prepare a clean draft.

4. **Editing:** Proofread narratives carefully; help others proofread; identify and correct mechanical errors.

5. **Publishing:** Publish writing in an appropriate form; share writing with an appropriate audience.

Section I: Writing for a Purpose and an Audience

Purpose: Am I writing to entertain? To inform? To persuade? To describe?

Audience: Am I writing for myself to express and clarify my ideas and/or feelings? Or am I writing for others? Possible audiences include my peers, younger children, parents, grandparents, children's authors, pen pals, etc.

Unit 1: Writing to Express Ideas

Purpose: Writing to learn and explore ideas and problems

Audience: Usually done for general, unknown audiences

Unit 2: Writing to Influence

Purpose: Writing to convince someone or sway his or her opinion to accept the writer's way of thinking

Audience: The audience may be known or unknown.

Unit 3: Writing to Inform

Purpose: Writing to share information with others

Audience: The audience may be known or unknown.

Unit 4: Writing to Entertain or Create

Purpose: Writing to create fictitious stories, true stories, poetry, or plays to entertain others

Audience: The audience may be classmates, family, or other trusted audiences.

Name: _____ Date: _____

Unit 1: Writing a Friendly Letter

Key Ideas
- A **friendly letter** is written to a person you know well.

- A friendly letter contains a **heading**, **greeting**, **body**, **closing**, and **signature**.

Practice

Directions: Read the friendly letter written below. Label the parts of the letter: heading, greeting, body, closing, and signature.

21825 Regency Rd.
Zap, ND 58580
February 8, 2001

Dear Kayte,

   How is your new school? Is it as nice as ours is? Have you made new friends? What are their names? I really miss you, especially at recess time. There just isn't anyone as much fun to play with as you.
   We are all doing fine here. Ms. Greene says we could use a winter break, though. She must mean we are getting too rowdy. We had a magician at our last assembly. It was neat. He pulled a bird out of his hat and handed it to Mr. Heyden. That was funny.
   I hope you are enjoying the lollipops in Lollipop, Texas. Ha ha. Write soon.

Your friend,

Julia (handwritten)

On Your Own: Write a friendly letter to someone you know well. Share your thoughts, news, or experiences with a friend or family member you don't see regularly. Be sure to include all the parts of a letter.

Name: _____ Date: _____

Unit 1: Writing a Business Letter

Key Ideas

- A **business letter** is like a friendly letter in that you must decide:
  - Who is my audience?
  - What is my purpose in writing?
  - What do I want to say?

- A **business letter** differs from a friendly letter in these ways:
  - A business letter also has an **inside address**. This is the address of the person to whom you are writing.
  - The greeting has a colon (:) after it, rather than a comma.
  - The closing is more formal (usually *Sincerely,* or *Yours truly,*).
  - The signature is typed as well as handwritten.

Practice

Directions: Read the business letter written below. Label the parts of the letter: heading, inside address, date, greeting, colon, body, closing, and signature.

20110 Grandview
Riverside, GA 12345
June 25, 2001

Mr. Bart Smith
Video Viewer
707 Salem Ave.
Scottville, IL 62683

Dear Mr. Smith:

Please send me a copy of your most recent video catalog. I am a big fan of your work. A check is enclosed for the cost of the catalog.

Sincerely,

Lateesha Brown (handwritten)

Lateesha Brown

On Your Own: Write a business letter to the CEO of a business in your community. Ask him or her to explain what the CEO of a company does.

Name: _____ Date: _____

Unit 1: Writing a Narrative

Key Ideas

- A **narrative** is a story that tells about something that happened. In a narrative, feelings are shared.

- A **narrative** is a story that contains:
  - a **topic sentence** that tells the main idea (what the author wants to say about the subject);
  - **supporting sentences** that give the details about what happens in the story; and
  - a **closing** that finishes the story.

Practice

Directions: Read the narrative story below. Identify the characteristics of a narrative by filling in the chart below.

The Day the Pig Got Loose

My family and I had been looking forward to visiting the state fair. While we were viewing the exhibits in the exhibit hall, a huge pig came running through the building. No one was more surprised than my mother. The pig started chasing her around the exhibits. I know she was scared, but she looked hilarious pushing my sister's stroller as she ran through the building. She was saved when she found the stairway and rushed up backwards, pulling the stroller behind her. This was a state fair our family will never forget!

Topic:	
Main Idea:	
Topic Sentence:	
Details:	
Closing Sentence:	

On Your Own: Write a narrative about the activities you and your best friend like to do together. Use a chart similar to the one above to plan your narrative.

Name: _____ Date: _____

Unit 1: Writing a Personal Narrative

Key Ideas
- A **personal narrative** is a true story that tells about something that happened to the person who tells it.

- **Personal narratives** have certain characteristics:
  - ❑ They grab the reader's attention right at the beginning.
  - ❑ They are told in first person using the pronoun "I."
  - ❑ They include important events in the order in which they happened.
  - ❑ They use details to tell what the author saw, heard, or felt.
  - ❑ They are told in the author's voice.
  - ❑ They have a satisfying ending that tells how the story worked out or how the author felt.

Practice

Directions: Read the personal narrative below. Decide if each of the characteristics above is met in this narrative. If "yes," put a check in the box before each characteristic.

The Bird Attack

"Quick, close the door before the bird gets in the house!" my father yelled. And just as quickly, my brother slammed the door—right on my father. The bird and my father were out on the porch with all the groceries. My brother and sister and I were all safe in the house. My father looked so surprised just before the door slammed that the three of us were laughing so hard we couldn't open the door to help him fight off the bird. We could hear him struggling with the bird and the groceries, and we did feel sorry for him. When we heard that it was quiet out on the porch, my brother slowly opened the door. There stood my father, not laughing, not even smiling. Oh, oh!

On Your Own: Write a short personal narrative on your own paper about a funny family experience you have had. Be sure to grab the reader's attention right from your first sentence.

Name: _____ Date: _____

Unit 1: Writing to Discover an Idea

Key Idea
- Writing can be used to discover what we think or to discover a good idea for writing.

Practice

Directions: On your own paper, you are going to write about a topic for two minutes without lifting up your pen or pencil. When your teacher says, "Go," start writing and keep writing until he or she says, "Stop!" If nothing comes to mind, write "my mind is blank" and keep writing. Your mind will eventually go back to the topic. Remember, don't lift your pen until your teacher calls, "Stop!"

Topic: What do you think should or could be done to stop the violence in schools?

Does everyone understand the topic? Get ready to write. Go!

(Call "Stop!" after two minutes.)

Reread what you've written, looking for the best sentence in the piece. When you find the best sentence, underline it. Rewrite that sentence at the top of a clean sheet of paper. When the teacher says, "Go," you will write about that sentence for one minute without stopping. Ready? Go!

(Call "Stop!" after one minute.)

Reread what you've written, looking for the best sentence in the piece. When you find the best sentence, underline it. Rewrite that sentence into a topic sentence. Be ready to share it with the class.

On Your Own: Use this technique whenever you need to explore ideas about a topic.

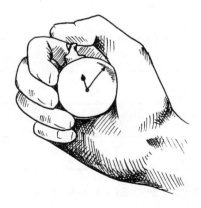

Name: _____ Date: _____

Unit 1: Writing to Solve a Problem

Key Idea
- **Writing** is helpful in solving problems. It often helps you figure out what to do.

Practice

Directions: Imagine you have been falsely accused of stealing school lunches from other students. How can you prove your innocence? Write out all of your ideas here:

_____

_____

_____

_____

_____

_____

_____

_____

_____

_____

_____

_____

_____

_____

_____

_____

_____

_____

On Your Own: Think about a problem you are having that you can't seem to solve. Write about it in as much detail as possible until you figure out a solution.

Name: _____ Date: _____

Unit 1: Writing a Journal

Key Idea
- **Journal writing** is a way of recording your private thoughts and ideas.

Practice

Directions: Read the journal prompt and write your response on the lines below. Decide if you wish to share your entry with others.

Journal Prompt: Explain how you clean your room when it is really a mess. What do you put away first? Do you usually have a plan? What do you like least about cleaning your room?

_____

_____

_____

_____

_____

_____

_____

_____

_____

_____

_____

_____

_____

_____

On Your Own: Choose one of these prompts to write about in your journal:
- What do you do for fun on weekends?
- Who is your hero? Why?
- Describe what makes you smile.
- What is your least favorite food?
- What really annoys you?

Name: _____ Date: _____

Unit 1: Writing a Reflection

Key Ideas

- A **reflection** is a thoughtful narrative about something of importance to the writer.

- A **reflection** follows the same format as a narrative:
  - a **topic sentence** that tells the main idea (what the author wants to say about the subject);
  - a **middle** that provides the details about how the writer feels or what the writer thinks; and
  - an **ending** that brings closure to the narrative.

Practice

Directions: Read the following reflection. Then answer the questions below.

A Sad Day

One of the saddest days of my life was when my dog Bailey died. I got Bailey as a puppy thirteen years ago, and we grew up together. She would wait by the back door for me to come home from school, and she would run with me when I played soccer. She was a good dog and a faithful friend.

1. Why is this considered a reflection? _____

   _____

2. Fill out the chart for the reflection.

Topic:	
Main Idea:	
Topic Sentence:	
Details:	
Closing Sentence:	

On Your Own: Think about an experience you have had that made you feel strongly. Were you angry? Sad? Happy? Confused? Frustrated? Write about this experience in a personal reflection in your journal or notebook.

Name: _____ Date: _____

Unit 1: Writing Skills Test

Directions: Darken the circle next to the choice that states the best answer.

1. When writing to express ideas, it is most important to know which one of these?
   ○ A. Who your audience is
   ○ B. What your supporting sentences are
   ○ C. What your closing is going to be
   ○ D. How old you are

2. When writing to express ideas, it is also important to know which one of these?
   ○ A. How to write paragraphs
   ○ B. How to write a complete sentence
   ○ C. What your purpose is
   ○ D. What your title is going to be

3. Finally, when writing to express ideas, it is also important to know which one of these?
   ○ A. The writing format you need
   ○ B. What you want to say
   ○ C. What you enjoy writing about
   ○ D. How long it will take you to write

4. Which of these describes a friendly letter?
   ○ A. A true story that happened to the author
   ○ B. A story that reports the feelings of the author
   ○ C. A letter written to request, inform, or complain, usually to someone the writer doesn't know
   ○ D. A letter written to a person the writer knows well

5. Which of these describes a business letter?
   ○ A. A true story that happened to the author
   ○ B. A story that reports the feelings of the author
   ○ C. A letter written to request, inform, or complain, usually to someone the writer doesn't know
   ○ D. A letter written to a person the writer knows well

6. Which of these describes a personal narrative?
   ○ A. A true story that happened to the author
   ○ B. A story that reports the feelings of the author
   ○ C. A letter written to request, inform, or complain, usually to someone the writer doesn't know
   ○ D. A letter written to a person the writer knows well

Name: _____ Date: _____

Unit 1: Writing Skills Test (cont.)

7. A narrative is a story that contains all but <u>one</u> of the following:
    - ○ A. A topic sentence that tells the main idea (what the author wants to say about the subject)
    - ○ B. Supporting sentences that give the details about what happens in the story
    - ○ C. A letter written to a person the writer knows well
    - ○ D. A closing that finishes the story.

8. Which of these is true for writing to discover an idea?
    - ○ A. It is a way to find out what you think or to find a good idea for writing.
    - ○ B. It is a way of recording your private thoughts and ideas.
    - ○ C. It is a way of helping you figure out a solution to a problem.
    - ○ D. It is a way to write thoughtfully about something of importance to you.

9. Which of these is true for writing to solve a problem?
    - ○ A. It is a way to find out what you think or to find a good idea for writing.
    - ○ B. It is a way of recording your private thoughts and ideas.
    - ○ C. It is a way of helping you figure out a solution to a problem.
    - ○ D. It is a way to write thoughtfully about something of importance to you.

10. Which of these is true for writing in a journal?
    - ○ A. It is a way to find out what you think or to find a good idea for writing.
    - ○ B. It is a way of recording your private thoughts and ideas.
    - ○ C. It is a way of helping you figure out a solution to a problem.
    - ○ D. It is a way to write thoughtfully about something of importance to you.

11. Which of these is true for writing a reflection?
    - ○ A. It is a way to find out what you think or to find a good idea for writing.
    - ○ B. It is a way of recording your private thoughts and ideas.
    - ○ C. It is a way of helping you figure out a solution to a problem.
    - ○ D. It is a way to write thoughtfully about something of importance to you.

Name: _____ Date: _____

Unit 1: Writing Skills Test (cont.)

12. Writing Sample 1:   **An Important Family Tradition**

- Write a narrative on the above topic. Before you begin writing, use scratch paper to brainstorm and organize your ideas. Use your imagination to make your writing colorful and interesting.

- Use the best English you can, but do not worry about mistakes. The most important thing is to be clear so that the person reading your writing can imagine what your family tradition is like.

_____

_____

_____

_____

_____

_____

_____

_____

_____

_____

_____

_____

_____

_____

_____

_____

_____

Name: _____ Date: _____

Unit 1: Writing Skills Test (cont.)

13. Writing Sample 2:   **Letter of Complaint**

- Write a letter of complaint to *The Disney Store* about a toy you purchased that broke, through no fault of yours. Before you begin writing, use scratch paper to brainstorm and organize your ideas.

- Use the best English you can, but do not worry about mistakes. The most important thing is to be clear so that the person reading your writing can understand what your complaint is and what you want the company to do about it.

_____

_____

_____

_____

_____

_____

_____

_____

_____

_____

_____

_____

_____

_____

_____

_____

_____

_____

Name: _____ Date: _____

Unit 2: Writing a Persuasive Essay

Key Ideas

- A **persuasive essay** is a narrative in which the writer argues on a topic he or she has strong beliefs and opinions about.

- In a **persuasive essay**, a writer introduces his or her argument, presents supporting reasons, draws conclusions, and convinces the reader to accept the writer's viewpoint.

Practice

Directions: What is something that your parents won't let you have? Do you want a pet? Do you want more television time? Do you want a later bedtime? Do you want a new bike? Draft an essay here that will persuade your parents to let you have what you want. Remember, your reasons must be convincing and your argument well supported. Use your own paper if you need more room.

_____

_____

_____

_____

_____

_____

_____

_____

_____

_____

_____

_____

_____

_____

On Your Own: Revise your persuasive essay, and type the final copy on a computer. Give it to your parents, and see if they are convinced.

Name: _____ Date: _____

Unit 2: Writing an Editorial

Key Ideas

- An **editorial** is a piece of persuasive writing intended to influence readers to the writer's viewpoint.

- An **editorial** has the following parts:
  - a **beginning** that states the writer's position or opinion;
  - a **middle** that contains at least three reasons for the writer's position or opinion; and
  - an **ending** that concludes the writing with a personal statement, a prediction, or a summary of the position.

Practice

Imagine that your local public school board is considering making a rule requiring all students to wear school uniforms. Write an editorial in which you take a position either for or against the rule. Remember to include all the necessary parts of an editorial.

_____

_____

_____

_____

_____

_____

_____

_____

_____

_____

_____

_____

On Your Own: What is an issue of importance at your school or in your community? Write an editorial for your local paper taking a position on the issue or stating your opinion. After careful editing, send your editorial to the newspaper.

Name: _____ Date: _____

Unit 2: Writing a Persuasive Letter

Key Ideas

- A **persuasive letter** is a letter that attempts to persuade the reader to do something or to stop doing something.

- There are three basic ways **to persuade people**:
  - Appeal to **reason** (e.g., giving them good, solid reasons for your argument);
  - Appeal to **character** (e.g., find someone they trust and use that person or the reputation of that person to support your argument);
  - Appeal to **emotions** (e.g., concern for their well-being, sense of responsibility, etc.).

Practice

Choose someone you know well and write a persuasive letter to him or her. You might write to your parents or grandparents arguing that they should stop smoking; a sibling or friend urging him or her not to take drugs; or a high school friend persuading him or her not to drink and drive. Remember, in order to persuade, you must appeal to at least one of the three basic ways to persuade people.

_____

_____

_____

_____

_____

_____

_____

_____

_____

_____

_____

On Your Own: Revise your letter, making it stronger. Make a final copy in your best handwriting, and send it to the person you are trying to persuade.

Name: _____ Date: _____

Unit 2: Writing a Letter to the Editor

Key Ideas

- A **letter to the editor** is a piece of persuasive writing intended to influence newspaper readers to the writer's viewpoint, giving at least three reasons to support the opinion.

- A **letter to the editor** is similar to an editorial but is written in letter form and can be on any issue of interest to the writer.

Practice

Directions: Read the following letter to the editor that appeared in a school newspaper. Answer the questions below on your own paper and decide how the writer is trying to influence or persuade you, the reader.

Dear Editor of South School News,

I am a fourth grader who has eaten almost 750 lunches in our school cafeteria. While the lunches provided are nutritious and filling, I would like to request a salad bar to be offered as well.

I think the salad bar would be appreciated by a lot of students. The fruits and vegetables on the salad bar would add more nutrition and variety to our lunch.

I'm sure there are rules and regulations regarding school lunches, but I would like the administration to consider offering a salad bar in our cafeteria.

David Hopping

---

1. How does the writer introduce his argument/opinion? Is it effective?

2. Does the writer give at least three reasons in support of his argument?

3. What are the reasons the writer gives for wanting the salad bar in the cafeteria?

4. How does the writer end his letter?

5. Does the writer convince you, the reader, of his argument? How?

On Your Own: Think about a problem in your school that you feel strongly about or would like to change. Or think about something that is very nice in your school that should stay. Develop a position on the matter, brainstorm at least three reasons to support your opinion, and draft a conclusion that contains either a personal statement, a prediction, or a summary of your argument. Put your letter to the editor in proper friendly letter form, proof it carefully, and send it to your school or local newspaper.

Name: _____ Date: _____

Unit 2: Writing a Letter of Request

Key Ideas

- A **letter of request**, like other persuasive writing, seeks to persuade the reader and asks something of the reader.

- A **letter of request** can be in a friendly letter format (if the writer knows the reader), or in a business letter format (if the writer doesn't know the reader).

Practice

Directions: Read the letter of request Kelly wrote to Freddie Prinze, Jr. Then answer the questions below on your own paper.

Freddie Prinze, Jr.,

  Hello, my name is Kelly, and I am twelve years old. I would just like to say what a huge fan I am of your movies. A bunch of my friends and I recently saw "Head Over Heels" at the theater. We absolutely loved it! Speaking of my friends, I have one very special friend, Joanna Bloese, who was diagnosed with leukemia about a year ago; she's a part of the "Make-A-Wish" Foundation. Joanna has just sent in her wish, which is to meet you. The problem is she found out that it can sometimes take almost a year for the wish to be granted. She is really worried that she won't make it that long, even though her doctors tell her not to worry. She keeps saying to herself over and over how she should've wished to meet you a year ago before she ran out of time. I know you probably get asked this question every day, and I know it's probably not likely or possible because you have such a busy schedule, but if you could meet with my friend as soon as you can, I know she would be so grateful. If it's not possible in any way at all to meet with her, then I'm sure that she'll understand because we know you're busy and everything. Thank you for listening to me, though, and no matter what happens, we will still love ya! Thanks again for listening. We'll see ya in the movies!

Sincerely,
Kelly

---

1. What is Kelly's request?

2. How does she introduce her request?

3. What reasons does she give to support her request?

4. Did she use the correct format for her letter of request?

5. How does she end her letter of request?

On Your Own: Do you have a friend who would benefit from the "Make-A-Wish" Foundation? If not, research the foundation on the Internet until you find someone who needs a friend like Kelly. Draft a letter of request for him or her.

Name: _____ Date: _____

Unit 2: Writing an Advertisement

Key Ideas
- An **advertisement** tells you about things you can buy, see, or do, and it is sometimes called an "ad" for short.

- An **ad** is like a written commercial for a person, place, thing, event, etc.

Practice

Directions: Read the following school advertisement. Then answer the questions below.

Arts and Crafts Fair
Michigan Avenue Elementary School

Arts, crafts, plants, baked goods, and more!
Things you want and stuff you didn't know you
needed are waiting for you at the
Arts and Crafts Fair!

For people of all ages
Thursday – Saturday
1:00 – 5:00
School Gym

1. What product or service is being advertised? _____

2. What does the writer use to persuade you to attend? _____

    _____

3. Has the writer persuaded you to attend? Why or why not? _____

    _____

4. How would you change the advertisement to make it more persuasive? _____

    _____

On Your Own: Write an ad for something you'd like to sell or an event you'd like people to know about. Remember to include all the pertinent information about the item or event without overwhelming people with details.

Name: _____ Date: _____

Unit 2: Writing Skills Test

Directions: Darken the circle next to the choice that states the <u>best</u> answer.

1. When writing to persuade, it is most important to know which one of these?
   - ○ A. What your opinion is
   - ○ B. How to write paragraphs
   - ○ C. What the story is
   - ○ D. What your title is going to be

2. Which of these <u>best</u> describes a persuasive essay?
   - ○ A. A letter in which the writer attempts to persuade the reader to do something or to stop doing something
   - ○ B. A letter written to the editor of a newspaper to influence the newspaper readers to the writer's viewpoint
   - ○ C. An essay in which the writer attempts to influence readers to the writer's viewpoint
   - ○ D. A written commercial for a person, place, thing, event, product, etc.

3. Which of these <u>best</u> describes a letter to the editor?
   - ○ A. A letter in which the writer attempts to persuade the reader to do something or to stop doing something
   - ○ B. A letter written to the editor of a newspaper to influence the newspaper readers to the writer's viewpoint
   - ○ C. An essay in which the writer attempts to influence readers to the writer's viewpoint
   - ○ D. A written commercial for a person, place, thing, event, product, etc.

4. Which of these <u>best</u> describes a persuasive letter?
   - ○ A. A letter in which the writer attempts to persuade the reader to do something or to stop doing something
   - ○ B. A letter written to the editor of a newspaper to influence the newspaper readers to the writer's viewpoint
   - ○ C. An essay in which the writer attempts to influence readers to the writer's viewpoint
   - ○ D. A written commercial for a person, place, thing, event, product, etc.

5. Which of these <u>best</u> describes an advertisement?
   - ○ A. A letter in which the writer attempts to persuade the reader to do something or to stop doing something
   - ○ B. A letter written to the editor of a newspaper to influence the newspaper readers to the writer's viewpoint
   - ○ C. An essay in which the writer attempts to influence readers to the writer's viewpoint
   - ○ D. A written commercial for a person, place, thing, event, product, etc.

Unit 2: Writing Skills Test (cont.)

6. Which of these <u>best</u> describes a request?
   - ○ A. An essay in which the writer attempts to influence readers to the editor's viewpoint
   - ○ B. An essay in which the writer attempts to influence readers to the writer's viewpoint
   - ○ C. A letter in which the writer asks for something from the reader
   - ○ D. A letter in which the writer attempts to persuade the reader to do something or to stop doing something

7. Which of these is true for writing a persuasive essay?
   - ○ A. The writer introduces the argument, presents supporting reasons, draws conclusions, and convinces the reader to accept the writer's viewpoint.
   - ○ B. It should contain twenty-nine sentences.
   - ○ C. It should be written in a friendly letter format.
   - ○ D. It should contain only three paragraphs.

8. Which of these is true for a persuasive letter?
   - ○ A. The writer introduces the argument, presents supporting reasons, draws conclusions, and convinces the reader to accept the writer's viewpoint.
   - ○ B. It should contain seven sentences.
   - ○ C. It should be written in paragraph format.
   - ○ D. It should contain at least one of three ways to persuade people.

9. Which of these statements <u>best</u> describes the purpose of persuasive writing?
   - ○ A. The audience might be known or unknown.
   - ○ B. Writing to argue logically with reasons to convince someone of something
   - ○ C. Includes essays, letters, advertisements, letters to the editor
   - ○ D. Writing to deceive or mislead the reader to convince him or her of something

Name: _____ Date: _____

Unit 2: Writing Skills Test (cont.)

10. Writing Sample 1:   **Living the Good Life**

- Where do you live? Do you like it? Would you like to live somewhere else? For example, if you live in the city, would you rather live in the country? If you live in the country, would you rather live in the city? Would you like to live in a different state? Would you like to live in a different house or apartment? Write a persuasive essay in which you either appeal to the reader's reason, appeal to the reader's character, or appeal to the reader's emotions to convince him or her that the good life would be living in _____.

- Before you begin writing, use scratch paper to brainstorm and organize your ideas. Use your imagination and sound reasoning to persuade your reader to accept your opinion. Make your writing lively and interesting.

- Use the best English you can, but do not worry about mistakes. The most important thing is to be clear so that the person reading your writing can understand your argument and follow the reasons for your opinion.

_____

_____

_____

_____

_____

_____

_____

_____

_____

_____

_____

_____

_____

_____

Name: _____ Date: _____

Unit 2: Writing Skills Test (cont.)

11.　Writing Sample 2:　**Letter of Request**

- A local newspaper has asked fourth graders to write letters nominating their mother, grandmother, aunt, or any other female relative for the "Outstanding Woman of the Year" Award, and you want to enter the contest. Write a letter of request to the newspaper committee asking them to choose your nominee as the winner.

- Before you begin writing, use scratch paper to brainstorm and organize your ideas. Use your imagination and reasoning to choose at least three important reasons to support your request. Make your writing interesting and colorful.

- Use the best English you can, but do not worry about mistakes. The most important thing is to be clear so that the person reading your request understands why it is important to accept your request.

_____

_____

_____

_____

_____

_____

_____

_____

_____

_____

_____

_____

_____

_____

_____

_____

Name: _____ Date: _____

Unit 3: Writing Instructions

Key Idea

- The purpose of **writing instructions** is to give clear, easy-to-follow directions in the order in which they are to be followed.

Practice

Suppose an Internet pal from another country asked you what a sandwich is and how to make one. What would you say? Think of your favorite sandwich and write step-by-step instructions in the outline below.

MY OUTLINE FOR MAKING A _____ **SANDWICH.**

Ingredients: _____   _____

_____   _____

Step One: _____

Step Two: _____

Step Three: _____

Step Four: _____

Step Five: _____

Special Instructions: _____

_____

Clean-up and/or safety concerns: _____

_____

Write the answers to the questions in the chart above.

1. Before you make a sandwich, what do you have to do or get?
   (*Example: Assemble all ingredients first.*)

2. What's the first step? Second step? Third step?

3. What comes next?

4. Then what do you do?

5. Are there more steps than five?

6. Have you mentioned cleaning up and/or safety concerns?

Did You Know? Sandwiches are named after the Earl of Sandwich.

Name: _____ Date: _____

Unit 3: Writing Instructions (cont.)

Now turn your sandwich outline from the previous exercise into an e-mail message to your Internet pal. Use the spell checker and grammar check on your computer to make sure you've edited all the errors.

| From: |
| To: |
| Date: |
| Subject: |

- Be sure to create a good introduction for your e-mail ... one that will "grab" your reader's attention.

- The middle of your e-mail should contain the instructions for making the sandwich.

- Have you given exact and clear instructions?

- Your e-mail would be more interesting if you could put in some facts about sandwiches.

- Have you ended your e-mail well or abruptly? Your ending should be satisfying to the reader.

The sandwich was born on August 6, 1762, at five o'clock in the morning. An Englishman named John Montague, the fourth Earl of Sandwich, was playing cards with his friends and didn't want to stop to eat, even though he was hungry. He ordered his servant to bring him some slices of roast beef between two slices of bread. And there you have it— the sandwich was born!

Other names for a sandwich: grinder, hero, submarine, gyro, wrap

Do you know any other names for a sandwich? List them.

_____

_____

_____

Name: _____ Date: _____

Unit 3: Writing a Description 1

Key Ideas

- **Writing a description** means creating with words a picture so clear that your readers can see what you see.

- **Descriptive writing** employs details to talk about a given subject.

Practice

1. It is important to use good descriptive adjectives when writing a description. Using a thesaurus or the Internet, find some *better* adjectives for the following overworked, tired adjectives.

   a. tall   -   towering, sky-high, large, giant
   b. small   -   _____
   c. red   -   _____
   d. messy -   _____

2. It is important to elaborate using details. Below is a sentence with few details. Rewrite it to include more details. You can use more sentences.

   I watched a movie.

   _____

   _____

   _____

   _____

   _____

   _____

   _____

   _____

   _____

   _____

On Your Own: Write a description of your bedroom at its messiest. Think about your senses: how does the room look, feel, smell, taste, sound? Use good descriptive adjectives to describe the mess. Use a synonym finder or a thesaurus to help you use a lot of details. Your description should be so clear that it would make any parent or guardian shudder!

Name: _____ Date: _____

Unit 3: Writing a Description 2

Key Ideas

- **Writing a description** means creating with words a picture so clear that your readers can see what you see.

- Use **descriptive adjectives** to create a clear picture of the person, place, or thing you are writing about.

Practice

Directions: Read the following paragraph and complete the activity below:

There is a mystery in your school. Someone is leaving candy on the students' desks when they leave the room. There is a rumor that it is a *teacher* in your school. Who could it be?

    Write a good description of one of the teachers in your school whom you suspect might be "The Candy Bandit." DO NOT mention this teacher's name. If your description is well-written, your classmates should be able to guess who you are describing. You should also be able to give a copy of your description to the teacher you describe.

_____

_____

_____

_____

_____

_____

_____

_____

_____

On Your Own: On your own paper, write a description of the person you most admire. Be sure to use descriptive adjectives to create a clear picture of that person.

Name: _____ Date: _____

Unit 3: Writing an Explanation

Key Ideas
- **Writing a description** means creating with words a picture so clear that your readers can see what you see.

- **Descriptive writing** employs details to talk about a given subject.

- An **explanation** is a reason for something. When writing an explanation for something, it is often important to employ details and use descriptive writing.

Practice

Directions: Imagine your teacher gave you an assignment to write an explanation for why you were late for school. Read Yolanda's explanation and complete the exercise below.

I was late for school because of a dog. It wasn't just any dog, but a tiny, white, fluffy puppy dog. I recognized her as Lucy, my neighbor's dog, and she looked so lonely and scared. Then she began following me to school. What could I do? I knew she was too small to find her way back home, and the street was so busy. I didn't want Lucy to get hurt, so I just had to take her back to Mrs. Chapman. I was late because I have a very soft spot for animals!

Now you try:

1. Write a sentence that tells why you were late. _____

   _____

   _____

   _____

2. Now add two details about your reason for being late: _____

   _____

   _____

   _____

Name: _____ Date: _____

Unit 3: Writing an Explanation (cont.)

3. Now add three descriptive adjectives to your details: _____

_____

_____

4. Add any other information that would make your explanation more descriptive, more interesting, or more colorful:

_____

_____

_____

5. Now create with words a picture so clear that your reader (your teacher) can see what you saw, feel what you felt, hear what you heard, and taste what you tasted. Write your finished descriptive explanation here:

_____

_____

_____

_____

_____

_____

_____

On Your Own: There are many uses for an explanation. Here are some:
- An explanation for not doing a chore or getting it finished on time
- An explanation for not doing well on a paper, project, or report card
- An explanation for making a mess

Choose one of these or one of your own and write a good descriptive explanation for something you did or didn't do. After editing and polishing it, give it to the person to whom it is owed.

Name: _____ Date: _____

Unit 3: Writing a Message

Key Ideas
- The purpose of writing a **message** to someone is to inform them of something.
- It is important when writing a **message** that you use clear, concise language.
- When writing a **message**, it is important that you separate main ideas from details.

Practice

Directions: Read the following message that Carlos wrote to his mother and answer the questions below.

> Mom,
>   I am going to study at Sam's house after school. Please pick me up at 5:00 P.M. He lives at 925 Rosemont Street. To get there, go to the elementary school, turn right and drive to the stop sign. At the stop sign, turn left (that is Rosemont Street). Go two blocks, then slow down. Sam's house is the only pink house on the left-hand side of the street.
>   Thanks, Mom.
>
>   Love,
>   Carlos

1. What is the purpose of Carlos's message? _____
_____

2. Is Carlos's message clear? _____

3. Will his mother have difficulty knowing what Carlos wants her to do? _____

4. Did he use clear, concise language? Give an example. _____
_____

5. Did he give too many details? _____

On Your Own: Now you try. Think of a message that you would like to send or give to someone. Remember that you want it to be as clear and concise as possible. You must be sure to give all the main ideas and as many details as necessary, but you don't want to give so many details that you overwhelm the reader. If you can't think of one, try one of these ideas.

- A message to a friend giving directions to your house
- A message to a family member about an important phone call
- A message to one of your brothers or sisters from your mother

Name: _____ Date: _____

Unit 3: Writing an Informational Paragraph

Key Ideas
- An **informational paragraph** is a paragraph that gives facts.

- The purpose of an **informational paragraph** is for the writer to share information about a topic he or she knows well.

Practice

> **The First Woman in Space**
> by J. D. Draw
>
> The first American woman in space was Sally Ride. She was one of only six women chosen as an astronaut in 1978. Sally went through tough training to be an astronaut. For example, she was dragged on a rope by a motorboat, then dropped 400 feet into the ocean. Sally Ride was also the youngest astronaut to go into orbit when she served as mission specialist in 1982 aboard the *Challenger*. The *Challenger* orbited the earth for six days.

1. What is the topic of the informational paragraph? _____

2. What is the main idea? _____

3. What are the facts? Underline them.

4. Does the author know the information well? How can you tell? _____

_____

_____

On Your Own: Write an informational paragraph about something that interests you. Use the following chart to help organize your information before writing. Some ideas for topics are a famous landmark, a favorite game or toy, or a place you'd like to visit.

Topic:	
Main Idea:	
Topic Sentence:	
Details:	
Conclusion:	

Name: _____ Date: _____

Unit 3: Writing an Individual Report

Key Ideas
- An **individual report** is a series of informational paragraphs about a topic of interest to the writer.

- An **individual report** involves authentic research to explore a topic or search for answers to questions of interest to the writer.

Practice

1. Choose a topic that interests you. A specific topic is more useful than a general one. For example, "Reptiles" is too general and covers too many areas, but "The Komodo Dragon" is specific enough for a report.   **Example**

    Your topic: _____   *The Komodo Dragon*

2. Write five points you want to learn about your topic:

    a. _____

    b. _____

    c. _____

    d. _____

    e. _____

What I want to know about Komodo Dragons:
a. Where do they live?
b. How big do they get?
c. What do they eat?
d. Are they dangerous to humans?
e. Is it really a dragon?

3. Arrange the five things you want to know in logical order.

    a. _____

    b. _____

    c. _____

    d. _____

    e. _____

a. What is a Komodo Dragon?
b. What do they look like; how big do they get?
c. Where do they live?
d. What do they eat?
e. Are they dangerous to humans?

3. Now find the answers to your questions by doing research. Look on the Internet at these addresses:

    www.yahooligans.com   Ask Earl
    www.ajkids.com   Ask Jeeves
    www.allexperts.com   Ask an Expert

For more information, you can look in encyclopedias, textbooks, or nonfiction books in your library, as well as in magazines and newspapers.

33

Name: _____ Date: _____

Unit 3: Writing an Individual Report (cont.)

Use note cards to write the answers to your questions and/or other important information. Use a different note card for each main idea or question. Be sure to write down where you found the information for each idea.

5. Make an outline from your note cards. Each question you asked will become a main topic. The information you researched will become the details that support the main topic.

    Example: I. The Komodo Dragon
                         II. The Size of Komodo Dragons
                         III. Where Komodo Dragons Can Be Found

6. Write a topic sentence for each main topic in your outline.

    Example: *What do they look like, and how big do they get?*
    Becomes: *Komodo Dragons are really lizards that can grow as long as ten feet.*

7. For each of the main topics, write an informational paragraph that includes interesting details.

8. Write an interesting, strong opening that tells the main idea of your report in one sentence. Ask a question or state a surprising fact to get your reader's attention.

9. Write a strong closing that sums up your report and that connects with the main idea in the opening. Leave your reader feeling satisfied.

10. At the end of your paper, make a list of your sources that shows exactly where you found your information.

11. Lastly, prepare a final, clean copy of your report for publication.

On Your Own: Follow the steps above to do another individual report on a topic of your choice or one assigned by your teacher.

Unit 3: Writing a Collaborative Report

Key Ideas
- A **collaborative report** is a report written by a group, each person contributing a section to the report. It is usually related to a thematic unit being studied.

- A **collaborative report** is beneficial because the work is shared.

Practice

1. **Choose a topic:** Choose a topic of interest from social studies, science, or current events. Some ideas include: oceans, dinosaurs, the universe, the Midwest, transportation, etc.

   Your topic: _____

2. **Design research questions:** What do you want to know about this topic? Brainstorm a list of questions, and write them on a chart or whiteboard. Add details to the questions.

3. What are your research questions? _____

   _____

   _____

   _____

4. **Gather and organize information:** Work in small groups or pairs to find the answers to your research questions. Gather information from a variety of resources, including the Internet, trade books, textbooks, encyclopedias, magazines, films, filmstrips, videotapes, etc. Use more than one source, but not more than one encyclopedia.

5. In your own words, write the answers to the questions you researched. _____

   _____

   _____

   _____

   _____

   _____

   _____

6. Organize the order in which you will write your information in your first draft.

7. **Draft the sections of the report.** Draft the separate sections of your report from the notes you took above. Remember, this is a rough draft, so content and ideas are more important at this time; the mechanics will come later. After your rough draft, share with the group and make revisions based on the feedback you receive.

Name: _____ Date: _____

Unit 3: Writing a Collaborative Report (cont.)

8. As a group, write an interesting introduction to the report that will "grab" your reader's attention right from the beginning.

9. As a group, write a strong ending that concludes or summarizes your report.

10. **Compile the sections:** Put all sections of the report together including the introduction, the ending, and the reference page. Edit the work carefully for grammar, spelling, and usage mistakes. Read the report aloud to find inconsistencies or redundant passages. Do one last revision.

11. **Publish the report:** Prepare a final copy with all revisions and editing completed. Type the final report on a word processor or computer and print out a final copy. Display in a book, on a bulletin board, or any other appropriate format.

On Your Own: If you liked this type of report writing, plan a classroom report where everyone in the class participates in the collaborative report. Here are some possible topics:

Women Scientists	Endangered Species	World Religions
Famous Mathematicians	Interesting Animals	States or Regions
Explorers Who Got Lost	Famous Inventions	African History
Washington, D.C., Monuments	World Holidays	Musical Instruments
The Seven Wonders of the World	Lands of the Far East	Tyrants of History

Name: _____ Date: _____

Unit 3: Writing Skills Test

Directions: Darken the circle next to the choice that states the <u>best</u> answer.

1. When writing instructions, which of these would be <u>most</u> important?
   - ○ A. To create word pictures so clear, your reader sees what you see
   - ○ B. To give clear, easy-to-follow directions in order
   - ○ C. To use a lot of details to talk about the subject
   - ○ D. To do authentic research to explore the topic

2. When writing a description, which of these would be <u>most</u> important?
   - ○ A. To create word pictures so clear, your reader sees what you see
   - ○ B. To give clear, easy-to-follow directions in order
   - ○ C. To use of lot of details to talk about the subject
   - ○ D. To do authentic research to explore the topic

3. When writing a report, which of these would be <u>most</u> important?
   - ○ A. To create word pictures so clear, your reader sees what you see
   - ○ B. To give clear, easy-to-follow directions in order
   - ○ C. To use of lot of details to talk about the subject
   - ○ D. To do authentic research to explore the topic

4. When writing an explanation, which of these would be <u>most</u> important?
   - ○ A. To create word pictures so clear, your reader sees what you see
   - ○ B. To give clear, easy-to-follow directions in order
   - ○ C. To use of lot of details to talk about the subject
   - ○ D. To do authentic research to explore the topic

5. When writing a message, which of these would be <u>most</u> important?
   - ○ A. To share information about a topic the writer knows well
   - ○ B. To search for answers to questions of interest to the writer
   - ○ C. To use clear, concise language to inform someone of something
   - ○ D. To write in collaboration with a group with each member contributing

6. When writing a collaborative report, which of these would be <u>most</u> important?
   - ○ A. To share information about a topic the writer knows well
   - ○ B. To search for answers to questions of interest to the writer
   - ○ C. To use clear, concise language to inform someone of something
   - ○ D. To write in collaboration with a group with each member contributing

7. When writing an informational paragraph, which of these would be <u>most</u> important?
   - ○ A. To share information about a topic the writer knows well
   - ○ B. To search for answers to questions of interest to the writer
   - ○ C. To use clear, concise language to inform someone of something
   - ○ D. To write in collaboration with a group with each member contributing

Name: _____ Date: _____

Unit 3: Writing Skills Test

8. When writing an individual report, which of these would be <u>most</u> important?
   - ○ A. To share information about a topic the writer knows well
   - ○ B. To search for answers to questions of interest to the writer
   - ○ C. To use clear, concise language to inform someone of something
   - ○ D. To write in collaboration with a group with each member contributing

9. Which of these <u>best</u> describes the purpose of the writing tasks in Unit 3?
   - ○ A. To learn and share information, one step at a time
   - ○ B. To write fictitious or true stories to entertain readers
   - ○ C. To argue logically with reasons to sway opinions
   - ○ D. To develop relationships and share information

10. When writing instructions, which of these would <u>not</u> be important?
   - ○ A. To give instructions, one step at a time
   - ○ B. To include enough details to make everything clear
   - ○ C. To write an interesting opening that gets the reader's attention
   - ○ D. To explain the purpose of the instructions

11. Which of these is <u>not</u> a characteristic of a good report?
   - ○ A. To research a topic of interest to you
   - ○ B. To include facts, not opinions
   - ○ C. To use your own words, not to copy someone else's
   - ○ D. To entertain your readers

Name: _____ Date: _____

Unit 3: Writing Skills Test (cont.)

12. Writing Sample 1:   **How to Play** _____

- Pretend the instructions to your favorite board or Internet game have been lost. Your task is to rewrite the instructions clearly so that someone who has never played the game before can play correctly.

- Before you begin writing, use scratch paper to brainstorm and organize your ideas. Think of your audience, your purpose, and how you will publish or share your information. Make sure you include all the steps in order and all the materials needed. Be sure details make each step clear.

- Use the best English you can, but do not worry about mistakes. The most important thing is to be clear and organized so your reader can follow your instructions.

_____

_____

_____

_____

_____

_____

_____

_____

_____

_____

_____

_____

_____

_____

_____

Name: _____ Date: _____

Unit 4: Writing a Story

Key Ideas

- A **story** is a narrative made up by the author.

- A **good story** has
  - a **beginning** (which sets up the plot, the setting, the characters)
  - a **middle** (which shows how the characters deal with the problem), and
  - an **end** (which shows how the characters solve the problem).

- An **interesting story** uses colorful detail and meaningful dialogue.

Practice

1. **Choosing a story idea.** List five ideas on the chart below that you could write about.

Who?	What?	Where?

2. **Discuss your story ideas with a partner.** Which idea does your partner think is best? Why? Which idea has the best beginning, middle, and end?

   a. _____

   b. _____

3. Do you have enough ideas for your story?   yes   no

4. Will this story interest your readers?   yes   no

5. Will you enjoy writing this story?   yes   no

Name: _____ Date: _____

Unit 4: Writing a Story (cont.)

6. Make a story map for your story.

BEGINNING

MIDDLE

END

7. **Write your story** on your own paper. Be sure to include events that are important to your main idea. Use time clues such as before, after, later, the next day, etc., to make the order clear.

Name: _____ Date: _____

Unit 4: Writing a Story—*Characters*

Key Ideas

- A **story** is a narrative made up by the author.

- A **good story** has
  - a **beginning** (which sets up the plot, the setting, the characters)
  - a **middle** (which shows how the characters deal with the problem), and
  - an **end** (which shows how the characters solve the problem).

- A **strong story** will have realistic, interesting characters.

Practice

Directions: Imagine an animal walking through the woods. He or she is new to the area and wants to make friends. Create your character.

1. What kind of animal is your main character? _____

2. What does your character look like? Describe your character's face, hair, body, clothes, and other features. How would you know your animal from others of his or her kind if you saw him or her?

   _____

   _____

   _____

   _____

3. What is your character's personality? Is he or she smart? Funny? Loud? Obnoxious? How would you know your character from others of his or her kind if you only heard him or her?

   _____

   _____

   _____

   _____

4. What are your character's feelings? Is he or she curious? Lonely? Fearful? Anxious? Brave?

   _____

   _____

   _____

Name: _____ Date: _____

Unit 4: Writing a Story—*Characters* (cont.)

5. How does your character act as he or she enters the woods or encounters other animals? Does he or she whistle bravely or shuffle fearfully? Blush bashfully? Pout stubbornly?

_____

_____

_____

_____

6. What are your character's interests? Does he or she play sports? Does he or she have a hobby? What interests does he or she have that makes your character different from the other animals?

_____

_____

_____

_____

7. Draw a picture of your character here:

Name: _____ Date: _____

Unit 4: Writing a Story—*Plot*

Key Ideas

- A **story** is a narrative made up by the author.

- A **good story** has
  - a **beginning** (which sets up the plot, the setting, the characters)
  - a **middle** (which shows how the characters deal with the problem), and
  - an **end** (which shows how the characters solve the problem).

- A **good story** has an interesting plot.

Practice

Directions: Develop your story here, using the character you created in the previous lesson and the following plot: **Your animal is walking in the woods and wants to meet new friends.**

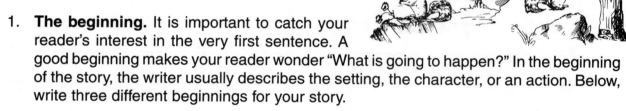

1. **The beginning.** It is important to catch your reader's interest in the very first sentence. A good beginning makes your reader wonder "What is going to happen?" In the beginning of the story, the writer usually describes the setting, the character, or an action. Below, write three different beginnings for your story.

   a. Begin by describing the setting: _____

   _____

   _____

   b. Begin by describing the character: _____

   _____

   _____

   c. Begin by describing an action: _____

   _____

   _____

   Put a check mark in front of the beginning you like the best.

2. **The middle.** The middle of your story includes only the events that are important to the main idea. What happens to your character as he or she walks in the woods? Is he or she successful in making friends? Does he or she experience problems? Get into trouble? Write the middle of your story on the next page. Be sure to use time clues to help your reader.

Unit 4: Writing a Story—*Plot* (cont.)

_____

_____

_____

_____

_____

_____

_____

_____

_____

_____

3. **The ending.** A good ending wraps up the story and makes the reader feel satisfied. There are no questions left unanswered, and it finishes the story. Write a good ending for your story here.

_____

_____

_____

_____

_____

On Your Own: Now draft your story of the animal walking in the woods wanting to make new friends. Describe your characters and their actions in a lively, interesting way so your audience will want to keep reading. End your story with a strong sentence that ties up all loose ends. There should be no unanswered questions.

Name: _____ Date: _____

Unit 4: Writing a Story—*Practice 1*

Key Ideas
- A **story** is a narrative made up by the author.

- A **good story** has
  - a **beginning** (which sets up the plot, the setting, the characters)
  - a **middle** (which shows how the characters deal with the problem), and
  - an **end** (which shows how the characters solve the problem).

- A **good story** has an interesting plot.

Practice

Directions: Choose one of the following writing prompts to create your own story. Use your own paper if you need more room.

- Imagine walking through a parking lot and finding a magic coin that would grant you three wishes.

- You are a mouse who could hide in very small places. Where do you hide?

- A terrible smell comes floating through the school. What is it?

- Create a story in which your desk at school suddenly starts to talk. What happens?

- What does the word *shiver* make you think of? Write a story in which the main character *shivers*.

_____

_____

_____

_____

_____

_____

_____

_____

_____

_____

_____

_____

_____

Name: _____ Date: _____

Unit 4: Writing a Story—*Practice 2*

Key Ideas

- A **story** is a narrative made up by the author.

- A **good story** has
  - a **beginning** (which sets up the plot, the setting, the characters)
  - a **middle** (which shows how the characters deal with the problem), and
  - an **end** (which shows how the characters solve the problem).

- A **good story** has an interesting plot.

Practice

Directions: Choose one of the following writing prompts to create your own story. Use your own paper if you need more room.

- Create a story with a superhero.

- Write a story about a character who finds a message in a bottle.

- Write a story about living on another planet one hundred years from now.

- Create a story in which you get to meet your favorite singer or group.

- Write a story about the new "family" that moved in next door.

_____

_____

_____

_____

_____

_____

_____

_____

_____

_____

_____

_____

Name: _____ Date: _____

Unit 4: Writing Poetry—*Formula Poems 1*

Key Ideas

- The purpose of **poetry** is to play with words, create images, explore ideas, and to entertain.

- Many types of **poetry** do not rhyme.

- Some **poetry** follows a format that provides a structure for the poet, but meaning is more important than form.

Practice: Formula Poems

1. Complete each line with a different wish to create this wish poem.

I Wish

I wish _____.

I wish _____.

I wish _____.

I wish _____.

I wish _____.

I wish _____.

I wish _____.

2. Now expand one wish into a poem with several lines, using your own paper if you need more room. Remember, your wish poem doesn't have to rhyme, but it should paint "word pictures" in the reader's mind.

_____

_____

_____

_____

_____

_____

_____

On Your Own: Read "I'm Thankful" by Jack Prelutsky (1984) and write a new version of it.

Name: _____　Date: _____

Unit 4: Writing Poetry—*Formula Poems 2*

Key Ideas

- The purpose of **poetry** is to play with words, create images, explore ideas, and to entertain.

- Many types of **poetry** do not rhyme.

- Some **poetry** follows a format that provides a structure for the poet, but meaning is more important than form.

Practice:　　Formula Poems

1.　Complete each line with a different description of the color *Green*.

Green

Green is _____.

Green is _____.

Green is _____.

Green is _____.

Green is _____.

Green is _____.

Green is _____.

2.　Now expand one line into a poem with several lines or stanzas, using your own paper if you need more room. Remember, your poem doesn't have to rhyme, but it should paint "word pictures" in the reader's mind.

_____

_____

_____

_____

_____

_____

_____

On Your Own: Write a formula poem about the five senses, or use the formula, "If I were ...", or " _____ is ...", or "I used to _____, but now _____"

Name: _____ Date: _____

Unit 4: Writing Poetry—*Free-Form Poems 1*

Key Ideas
- The purpose of **poetry** is to play with words, create images, explore ideas, and to entertain.

- Many types of **poetry** do not rhyme.

- **Free-form poems** express a thought or tell a story without concern for rhyme, repetition, or other patterns.

Practice: Free-Form Poems

1. Use a few well-chosen words (less than 20) to describe one of these emotions: *fear, loneliness, joy, sadness, embarrassment, enthusiasm.*

_____

_____

_____

_____

_____

_____

2. Brainstorm some ways you enjoy your days off from school.

When I Don't Have School ...

_____

_____

_____

_____

_____

_____

_____

_____

Name: _____ Date: _____

Unit 4: Writing Poetry—*Free-Form Poems 2*

Key Ideas

- The purpose of **poetry** is to play with words, create images, explore ideas, and to entertain.

- Many types of **poetry** do not rhyme.

- **Free-form poems** express a thought or tell a story without concern for rhyme, repetition, or other patterns.

Practice: Free-Form Poems

1. Read this poem by Robin. Notice how he has combined art and writing.

> **Your Time is Running Out**
> By Robin
>
> Your time is running out
> But where is it going?

2. Read this concrete poem by Kayte. Notice how she has used the words of her poem to create a picture.

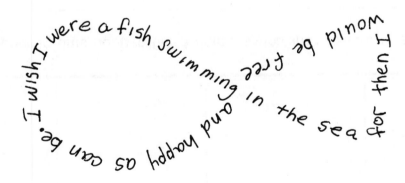

3. On your own paper, put your words together in a free-form poem that expresses a thought or tells a story.

On Your Own: Write a "found" poem. Create a poem from a newspaper or magazine article. Circle all of the important, interesting, and colorful words. Rearrange the words, add words, or delete words to form a poem.

Name: _____ Date: _____

Unit 4: Writing a Play—*Dialogue 1*

Key Ideas
- Passages of talk in a play or story are called **dialogue**.
- When writing **dialogue**, it is important to put quotation marks around a speaker's exact words.

Practice

1. Write a simple dialogue between you and a parent in which you are asking for a later bedtime.

   YOU: _____

   _____

   PARENT: _____

   _____

   YOU: _____

   _____

   PARENT: _____

   _____

2. Now draw a picture of your conversation using cartoon strip balloons in the boxes below.

On Your Own: Write a dialogue between a baseball and a bat just before the pitcher releases the ball.

Name: _____ Date: _____

Unit 4: Writing a Play—*Dialogue 2*

Key Ideas

- Passages of talk in a play or story are called **dialogue**.

- When writing **dialogue**, it is important to put quotation marks around a speaker's exact words.

Practice

1. Imagine two people witnessing a robbery. They are trying to describe the experience and the robbers to the policewoman, but they have very different stories. Write the dialogue here.

_____

_____

_____

_____

_____

_____

_____

_____

_____

_____

_____

_____

_____

_____

_____

_____

On Your Own: Write a dialogue between you and a toy that can talk.

Name: _____ Date: _____

Unit 4: Writing a Play

Key Ideas
- Passages of talk in a play or story are called **dialogue**.

- When writing **dialogue**, it is important to put quotation marks around a speaker's exact words.

Practice

1. **Finding an idea.** Think about the audience for your play, then choose a story that will interest or entertain them. Choose one of these ideas for your play or think up one of your own:
    - A favorite story or scene from a book
    - An exciting experience you had
    - A surprising experience you had
    - Describe a make-believe adventure

   Your idea for a play: _____

2. **Planning your play.** Just like a story, a play has a beginning, a middle, and an end. Like a story, a play has interesting characters, a colorful setting, and a plot that includes a problem. Plan your play using the chart below.

Characters	Setting	Plot
		Beginning:
		Middle:
		End:

Name: _____ Date: _____

Unit 4: Writing a Play (cont.)

3. **Writing your play.** List your characters, props, setting, and stage directions first. The stage directions tell the actors what actions to take during the play. The characters perform actions and talk; therefore, your dialogue must be realistic. End your play in a way that wraps up the action. Use your own paper if you need more room.

_____

_____

_____

_____

_____

_____

_____

_____

_____

_____

_____

_____

_____

_____

_____

_____

_____

On Your Own: Ask your classmates to read the play aloud. Make corrections. Choose actors and perform your play for an audience.

Name: _____ Date: _____

Unit 4: Writing Skills Test

Directions: Darken the circle next to the choice that states the <u>best</u> answer.

1. Which of these is <u>not</u> a characteristic of a good story?
   - ○ A. It has a beginning, a middle, and an end.
   - ○ B. It is made up by the author and is usually not true.
   - ○ C. It has interesting characters.
   - ○ D. It is written to be performed on a stage for an audience.

2. Which of these describes what a story is?
   - ○ A. It is a narrative made up by the author.
   - ○ B. It is an arrangement of words that creates images.
   - ○ C. It is passages of talk in a narrative.
   - ○ D. It is a narrative written to be performed on a stage for an audience.

3. Which of these describes a poem?
   - ○ A. It is a narrative made up by the author.
   - ○ B. It is an arrangement of words that creates images.
   - ○ C. It is passages of talk in a narrative.
   - ○ D. It is a narrative written to be performed on a stage for an audience.

4. Which of these describes dialogue?
   - ○ A. It is a narrative made up by the author.
   - ○ B. It is an arrangement of words that creates images.
   - ○ C. It is passages of talk in a narrative.
   - ○ D. It is a narrative written to be performed on a stage for an audience.

5. Which of these describes a play?
   - ○ A. It is a narrative made up by the author.
   - ○ B. It is an arrangement of words that creates images.
   - ○ C. It is passages of talk in a narrative.
   - ○ D. It is a narrative written to be performed on a stage for an audience.

6. When thinking of writing a story, which of these would you do first?
   - ○ A. Write the story.
   - ○ B. Discuss ideas with a partner.
   - ○ C. Choose an interesting idea.
   - ○ D. Write a good plot.

Name: _____ Date: _____

Unit 4: Writing Skills Test (cont.)

7. Which of these would <u>not</u> be an especially important question if you were going to write a story?
    ○ A. Do you have enough ideas for your story?
    ○ B. Have you made a map of your story?
    ○ C. Will this story interest your readers?
    ○ D. Will you enjoy writing about this story?

8. A story contains all but which <u>one</u> of the following?
    ○ A. Interesting, believable characters
    ○ B. A setting that tells when and where the story takes place
    ○ C. A plot that focuses on the main problem in the story
    ○ D. Stage directions

9. All but <u>one</u> of these describes a good ending for a story. Which one <u>doesn't</u>?
    ○ A. Shows how the characters deal with the problem
    ○ B. Shows how the characters solve the problem
    ○ C. Leaves the reader satisfied
    ○ D. Ties up all loose ends and leaves no unanswered questions

10. Which of these best describes the purpose of poetry?
    ○ A. To play with words, create images, explore ideas, and to entertain
    ○ B. To record personal experiences
    ○ C. To develop relationships and share information
    ○ D. To draw generalizations about life

11. Which of these is true for writing dialogue?
    ○ A. It is important that it rhymes.
    ○ B. It is important that it be between two people.
    ○ C. It is important to put quotation marks around the speaker's exact words.
    ○ D. It is important to entertain the audience.

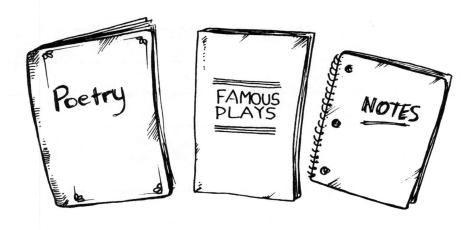

Name: _____ Date: _____

Unit 4: Writing Skills Test (cont.)

12. Writing Sample 1:   **A Strange Disappearance**

- Write a story about a strange disappearance. Before you begin writing, use scratch paper to brainstorm and organize your ideas.

- Use the best English you can, but do not worry about mistakes. The most important thing is to be clear so your reader can understand what happens in your story.

_____

_____

_____

_____

_____

_____

_____

_____

_____

_____

_____

_____

_____

_____

_____

_____

_____

Name: _____ Date: _____

Unit 4: Writing Skills Test (cont.)

13. Writing Sample 2:   **If I Were Something Else**

- Write a poem about how you would feel and what you would do if you were something else—like a dinosaur, a hot dog, or a rain cloud, for example. Begin your poem with "If I were ...". Before you begin writing, use scratch paper to brainstorm and organize your ideas.

- Use the best English you can, but do not worry about mistakes. The most important thing is to use wordplay, a poetic form, or a poetic device in your poem.

_____

_____

_____

_____

_____

_____

_____

_____

_____

_____

_____

_____

_____

_____

_____

_____

_____

Name: _____ Date: _____

Unit 5: Choosing the Proper Format for Writing

Key Ideas
- It is important to use written language for a variety of audiences and purposes and in a variety of **writing formats**.

- It is important to be able to choose the appropriate **format** for your writing purpose, including journals, letters, reviews, poems, narratives, and instructions.

Practice

friendly letter	**business letter**	**persuasive letter**
narrative	**personal narrative**	**journal**
persuasive essay	**instructions**	**poem**
advertisement/commercial	**editorial**	**book review**
description	**explanation**	**message**
informational paragraph	**individual report**	**story**
collaborative report	**play**	**letter of request**

Directions: From the list of writing formats covered in this book, choose the one from the word bank above that would be most appropriate for each of these writing assignments.

1. An exciting soccer game I played _____

2. Why we need a new school _____

3. The moon _____

4. *The Magic Feather* _____

5. Things seem to go wrong no matter what I do _____

6. E-mail to an Internet pal _____

7. Reason for not having your book for class _____

8. Request for an autograph _____

9. The school carnival _____

10. My best friend _____

Name: _____ Date: _____

Unit 5: Choosing the Proper Format for Writing (cont.)

Directions: Choose a favorite fairy tale (e.g., Cinderella, Hansel and Gretel, Jack and the Beanstalk, Beauty and the Beast, Snow White, etc.). Write the story in four different formats as indicated below.

A friendly letter: _____

_____

_____

_____

_____

_____

_____

_____

_____

_____

_____

An informational paragraph: _____

_____

_____

_____

_____

_____

_____

_____

_____

_____

_____

_____

Name: _____ Date: _____

Unit 5: Choosing the Proper Format for Writing (cont.)

A message: _____

_____

_____

_____

_____

_____

_____

_____

_____

_____

_____

_____

A journal entry: _____

_____

_____

_____

_____

_____

_____

_____

_____

_____

_____

_____

Name: _____ Date: _____

Unit 5: Writing Skills Test

Directions: Darken the circle next to the choice that states the best answer.

1. If I wanted to write and thank my grandmother for the socks she sent me, which format would I use?
   - ○ A. A business letter
   - ○ B. A persuasive letter
   - ○ C. A friendly letter
   - ○ D. A journal entry

2. If I wanted to remember my thoughts and feelings the day my cat died, which format would I use?
   - ○ A. A business letter
   - ○ B. A persuasive letter
   - ○ C. A friendly letter
   - ○ D. A journal entry

3. If I wanted to write for the ingredients of Coke™, which format would I use?
   - ○ A. A business letter
   - ○ B. A persuasive letter
   - ○ C. A friendly letter
   - ○ D. A journal entry

4. If I wanted to write and convince someone to vote for my candidate, which format would I use?
   - ○ A. A business letter
   - ○ B. A persuasive letter
   - ○ C. A friendly letter
   - ○ D. A journal entry

5. If I wanted to write about how to do something, which format would I use?
   - ○ A. Descriptive writing
   - ○ B. A message
   - ○ C. A story
   - ○ D. Instructions

6. If I wanted to write a prediction about the future, which format would I use?
   - ○ A. Descriptive writing
   - ○ B. A message
   - ○ C. A story
   - ○ D. Instructions

Name: _____ Date: _____

Unit 5: Writing Skills Test (cont.)

7. If I wanted to write about a picture I saw in a magazine, which format would I use?
   ○ A. Descriptive writing
   ○ B. A message
   ○ C. A story
   ○ D. Instructions

8. If I wanted to write down a telephone call for my father, which format would I use?
   ○ A. Descriptive writing
   ○ B. A message
   ○ C. A story
   ○ D. Instructions

9. If I wanted to write what I learned about the Stanley Cup, which format would I use?
   ○ A. An informational paragraph
   ○ B. A collaborative report
   ○ C. An individual report
   ○ D. A persuasive essay

10. If I wanted to write about why smoking is bad for your health and convince you to quit smoking, which format would I use?
    ○ A. An informational paragraph
    ○ B. A collaborative report
    ○ C. An individual report
    ○ D. A persuasive essay

11. If my group wanted to write about different kinds of dinosaurs, which format would I use?
    ○ A. An informational paragraph
    ○ B. A collaborative report
    ○ C. An individual report
    ○ D. A persuasive essay

12. If I wanted to write about the invention of Lincoln Logs™, which format would I use?
    ○ A. An informational paragraph
    ○ B. A collaborative report
    ○ C. An individual report
    ○ D. A persuasive essay

Name: _____ Date: _____

Unit 5: Writing Skills Test (cont.)

13. Writing Sample 1:   **How to** _____

- In this writing sample, you will write about how to do something. Before you begin writing, use scratch paper to list all the steps you should take, then organize them in order from the first to the last.

- Use the best English you can, but do not worry about mistakes. The most important thing is to describe every step in the correct order. Use the notes you made on the scratch paper to stay organized. Some possible ideas: how to make a French braid, how to play a sport, how to create a website, how to pitch a tent, how to make cookies, etc.

_____

_____

_____

_____

_____

_____

_____

_____

_____

_____

_____

_____

_____

_____

_____

_____

Section II: Conventions of Writing—*Introduction*

It is important in writing to clearly communicate your message. To accomplish this, you must use the **conventions of writing**—that is, the established rules of grammar, spelling, punctuation, capitalization, and usage for the English language.

Grammar - the study of the rules of a language or how the language works.

- This includes the study of patterns of a language: how words fit together to form phrases, how phrases fit together to make clauses, and how clauses fit together to form sentences.

- It is important to correctly use nouns, pronouns, verbs, adjectives, and adverbs in your writing. Subjects and predicates make up sentences and are made up of nouns, pronouns, and verbs. Adjectives and adverbs make your writing more interesting and colorful.

Spelling - the study of the order of the letters that make up a word.

- It is important to use "conventional" spelling—that is, to spell words the way readers expect the words to be spelled (not necessarily how they sound) to help communicate your meaning.

Punctuation - the purpose of punctuation is to clarify the meaning of the message for the reader.

- Punctuation marks, such as commas, periods, apostrophes, exclamation marks, question marks, and so on, help the writer communicate his or her meaning clearly.

Usage - the correct use of words and phrases that are frequently misused in writing.

- Correct usage communicates the exact meaning of the writer.

As you can see from the definitions of the conventions of writing, all of the parts need attention if the writer is to clearly and exactly communicate his or her message to the reader. English is a complicated language, and it takes study and hard work to improve knowledge and skill in the conventions. By practicing and applying the knowledge and skills on the activity sheets included in this section, you will become a better writer.

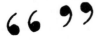

Name: _____ Date: _____

Unit 6: Capitalizing Proper Nouns

Key Ideas

- A **proper noun** is a noun that names a *particular* person, place, or thing.

- **Proper nouns** are capitalized.

- If there is more than one word in the **proper noun,** capitalize each important word.

Practice

Directions: Read the following sentences carefully. Pay special attention to the underlined nouns. If they are proper nouns and need to be capitalized, write them correctly on the lines below. If the sentence is correct, write "correct" on the line.

1. The first <u>men's world cup</u> was won by <u>uruguay</u> in 1930.

   _____

2. Aunt Kathleen and <u>uncle</u> Jeremy went to <u>france</u> last fall.

   _____

3. The <u>championship game</u> between the <u>wildcats</u> and the <u>tigers</u> was really exciting.

   _____

4. Mom and <u>dad</u> are taking us to the <u>illinois state fair</u> next week.

   _____

5. Our class went on a field trip to the <u>art museum</u> in Chicago.

   _____

6. Mrs. Sanchez teaches <u>math</u>, <u>english</u>, and <u>spanish</u> at our school.

   _____

7. The <u>maple leaf</u> is the symbol on the <u>flag of canada</u>.

   _____

8. I think <u>mr. williamson</u> lives at 3344 South <u>sycamore</u> Street.

   _____

9. We had to read *<u>the diary of a young girl</u>* for our history class.

   _____

10. Did you enjoy the <u>band concert</u> yesterday?

    _____

Name: _____ Date: _____

Unit 6: Capitalizing Proper Nouns (cont.)

Directions: Read the following sentences carefully. Underline each noun. If the noun is a proper noun and should be capitalized, use the proofreader's mark (⹀) to show this.

Example: The women's soccer team from the <u>united</u> <u>states</u> is great.

On July 10, 1999, the United States women's soccer team defeated china to win the 1999 world cup. The game was held at the rose bowl in pasadena, california, in front of a crowd of 90,185 people. This was the largest crowd to ever attend a women's sporting event in the united states. The game ended in a 0–0 tie, so the game had to be decided by a shoot-out. China kicked first and made 4 of 5 penalty kicks. The U.S. team made their first four kicks. It was all up to brandi chastain. If she made her shot, the united states would bring home the championship. Brandi's high, hard kick sailed to the top of the net over the head of the goalie, winning the shoot-out by a score of 5–4. Her teammates and the crowd were thrilled!

The women's world cup has been held three times, in 1991, 1995, and 1999. The united states has won twice, in 1991 and 1999. The next tournament is scheduled for 2003. The people of the united states hope the team wins again.

On Your Own: Write a personal narrative about an exciting game you watched or participated in. Who were the players? What was the game? Where was the game? What made it so exciting? Be sure to capitalize all the proper nouns in your narrative.

Name: _____ Date: _____

Unit 6: Capitalizing Initial Words in Sentences

Key Idea
- Use a **capital letter** to begin the first word in every sentence.

Practice

Directions: Write a sentence in which you describe each of these favorites and tell why it is your favorite. Be sure to use capital letters correctly. Try to begin each sentence differently.

1. Your favorite soft drink: _____

    _____

2. Your favorite superhero: _____

    _____

3. A teacher you admire: _____

    _____

4. A product you would recommend: _____

    _____

5. A person you would help: _____

    _____

6. A movie or recording star you would like to meet: _____

    _____

7. Your favorite kind of pizza: _____

    _____

8. A book that you read and really liked: _____

    _____

9. Your favorite television show: _____

    _____

10. A subject in school that you really enjoy: _____

    _____

On Your Own: Imagine that your spaceship touched down on an alien planet. When you get out of the spaceship, you meet ten talking aliens. Write a story, using dialogue, that describes your experience. Be sure to begin each sentence with a capital letter.

Name: _____ Date: _____

Unit 6: Capitalizing Titles and Abbreviations

Key Ideas

- Begin a **title** with a capital letter.

- Capitalize each important word in a **title**.

- Begin each **abbreviation** for a proper noun or title with a capital letter.

Practice

Directions: Rewrite each of the sentences below, capitalizing the titles and abbreviations correctly.

1. dr. smith delivered a baby girl named marie to the brown family on oak ave.

    _____

    _____

2. j k rowling is the author of *harry potter and the sorcerer's stone.*

    _____

    _____

3. mrs elena moreno lives at 406 chicago dr.

    _____

    _____

4. mr buffington read the poem "casey at the bat" to our class today.

    _____

    _____

5. i wonder why cassandra and mitchell didn't come to see our play, *a christmas carol.*

    _____

    _____

On Your Own: Write the names of ten good children's books and the name of the person or persons who wrote each one. Be sure to use capitalization correctly.

Name: _____ Date: _____

Unit 6: Capitalizing Days and Months

Key Ideas

- **Capitalize** the days of the week, the months of the year, and holidays.

- **Do** *not* **capitalize** the seasons.

> **Example:** Labor Day, the last holiday of summer, falls on the first
> Monday in September.

Practice

Directions: Rewrite each of the sentences below, capitalizing the days and months correctly.

1. At tuesday's meeting, rev. martin scheduled the church picnic for memorial day.

   _____

   _____

2. señora hernandez told us that cinco de mayo is celebrated on may 5 in los angeles.

   _____

   _____

3. on wednesday afternoon, i had an appointment with dr. jones, our dentist.

   _____

   _____

4. thanksgiving day is celebrated on the fourth thursday in november.

   _____

   _____

5. The last day of church camp this summer will be friday, august 18.

   _____

   _____

On Your Own: When were you born? Write a complete sentence that tells the day of the week, the date, month, and year. What season was it? Use capitalization correctly.

Name: _____ Date: _____

Unit 6: Capitalizing Academic Subjects and Languages

Key Idea
- The only school subjects that are **capitalized** are languages and specific place names used as modifiers.

    Example: Next year our school will offer Japanese, German, English literature, mathematics, biology, history, and Chinese philosophy.

Practice

Directions: For each of the sentences, write the words that should be capitalized on the line below each sentence. If the sentence is correct, write "correct" on the line.

1. I am not taking french next year because I didn't do well in that class this year.

   _____

2. My biology teacher never gives tests on fridays.

   _____

3. My aunt and uncle, who are of german heritage, never celebrate thanksgiving day.

   _____

4. mr. yoko, my japanese teacher, is very strict.

   _____

5. I think mathematics is the hardest subject I take.

   _____

6. melissa and i are taking european history next year.

   _____

7. Pham has graciously offered to tutor me in physics and english.

   _____

8. My mathematics teacher said that my grades were good enough to take algebra.

   _____

9. Señora melba will again be my spanish teacher.

   _____

10. After all these classes, i'm going to be hungry for some french fries!

   _____

On Your Own: Make a list of all the subjects you now study in school and another list of all those you think you will have to study in high school. Be sure to capitalize correctly.

Name: _____ Date: _____

Unit 6: Capitalizing Quotations

Key Ideas

- **Capitalize** the first word of a quoted sentence.

  Example: Mother said, "Do not forget to clean your room."

- **Do *not* capitalize** the first word within quotation marks if it does not begin a complete sentence.

  Example: "I am tired of waiting," Mother said, "for you to clean your room!"

Practice

Directions: Rewrite each of the sentences below, capitalizing words correctly.

1. Senator john dankin, a leading figure in the republican party, said, "we will win!"

   _____

   _____

2. "history will come alive," said miss thomas, our asian history teacher.

   _____

   _____

3. "The birds are flying south," our biology teacher said, "because winter is on its way."

   _____

   _____

4. "how many students are in your class this year?" asked jamie.

   _____

   _____

5. "zack is the best batter on his team," I said, "and he's also a good pitcher."

   _____

   _____

On Your Own: Write the *exact* words your mother, father, or grandparent has said to you a thousand times. Use a broken quote (as in number 3 above), and be sure to capitalize correctly.

Name: _____ Date: _____

Unit 6: Capitalizing Directions

Key Ideas

- **Capitalize** the points of a compass only when referring to a specific place or region (i.e., when it is a proper noun).

   Example: We go to South School.

- **Do *not* capitalize** the directions when the compass points refer to direction.

   Example: We were walking north to go to South School.

Practice

Directions: For each of the sentences, decide if each compass point and any proper nouns should be capitalized. If so, put the editor's mark ($\equiv$) below the letter of each word that should be capitalized. If the sentence is correct, no mark is needed.

1. Jeff said he would be late because he was north of the highway.

2. Marco has been living in south boston for over twenty-five years.

3. "I am not going into west l.a.," the salesman said. "It is too far away."

4. My family is going south for the winter; we are visiting south florida.

5. My sister's kindergarten teacher, ms. watson, has been at north school for ten years.

6. The civil war was between the north and the south.

7. "First you go north, then three miles east," my mother said, "and then go 2.5 miles to the south service station and ask for more directions!"

8. "Did you see the pictures," dr. burton asked Mike, "of the erupting volcano out west?"

9. Maria's parents are going out east to visit her grandparents.

10. During the 1800s, many people traveled to the west in covered wagons.

On Your Own: Write a sentence that contains all four compass points but only two of them are used as directions. Share your sentence with others in your class.

Name: _____ Date: _____

Unit 6: Capitalization Test

Directions: Read each sentence. Darken the circle next to the choice that is the correct way to capitalize the word or group of words that goes in the blank.

1. My dad played a good trick on my mom on _____.
   - ○ A. april fool's day
   - ○ B. April fool's Day
   - ○ C. April Fool's Day
   - ○ D. April fool's day

2. My favorite book is _____.
   - ○ A. *James and the giant peach*
   - ○ B. *James and the Giant Peach*
   - ○ C. *james and the giant peach*
   - ○ D. *James and the Giant peach*

3. We saw planets, stars, and galaxies at the _____.
   - ○ A. St. Louis Science Center
   - ○ B. St. Louis science center
   - ○ C. St. louis science center
   - ○ D. st. louis science center

4. Jasmine comes from a small city in _____.
   - ○ A. south florida
   - ○ B. south Florida
   - ○ C. South Florida
   - ○ D. South florida

5. _____ we will take our field trip to the history museum.
   - ○ A. next month
   - ○ B. Next month
   - ○ C. Next Month
   - ○ D. next Month

6. My son _____ lives in a big apartment.
   - ○ A. from New York City
   - ○ B. from new York City
   - ○ C. from New York city
   - ○ D. From new york city

7. My teacher, _____, is thinking about retiring.
   - ○ A. mr. t. h. taylor
   - ○ B. Mr. T. H. taylor
   - ○ C. Mr. T. H. Taylor
   - ○ D. Mr. t. h. Taylor

Name: _____ Date: _____

Unit 6: Capitalization Test (cont.)

8. _____ have a big cat named Tiny.
   - ○ A. Pham and naman
   - ○ B. pham and Naman
   - ○ C. Pham And Naman
   - ○ D. Pham and Naman

9. _____ I was late because of my dentist appointment.
   - ○ A. On Wednesday
   - ○ B. on Wednesday
   - ○ C. On wednesday
   - ○ D. on wednesday

10. My friend Nathan lives on _____.
    - ○ A. Chicago St.
    - ○ B. chicago st.
    - ○ C. Chicago st.
    - ○ D. chicago St.

11. _____ is the first holiday of the summer.
    - ○ A. Memorial Day
    - ○ B. Memorial day
    - ○ C. memorial Day
    - ○ D. memorial day

12. Monty is brave enough to take _____ with me next year.
    - ○ A. european history
    - ○ B. European history
    - ○ C. European History
    - ○ D. european History

13. Barbara wanted me to join the _____.
    - ○ A. girl scouts of america
    - ○ B. Girl Scouts of America
    - ○ C. Girl scouts of America
    - ○ D. girl scouts of America

14. My teacher said, "_____ to put your name on your paper."
    - ○ A. don't forget
    - ○ B. Don't forget
    - ○ C. Don't Forget
    - ○ D. don't Forget

15. Our school received a grant for twenty _____ and some software.
    - ○ A. apple™ computers
    - ○ B. apple™ Computers
    - ○ C. Apple™ computers
    - ○ D. Apple™ Computers

76

Name: _____ Date: _____

Unit 7: Punctuation—*Sentences*

Key Ideas
- A sentence that is a statement or a command ends with a **period (.)**.
- A sentence that is a question ends with a **question mark (?)**.
- A sentence that is an exclamation ends with an **exclamation point (!)**.

Practice

Directions: Read each sentence, decide what kind of punctuation is needed, then add it to the sentence.

1. What a wonderful surprise

2. I wasn't expecting you until Tuesday

3. Did you get an early start on your drive

4. How was the trip

5. We are so glad you made it safely

6. We have many things planned for your visit

7. Wow, you brought a lot of suitcases

8. How long are you planning to stay

9. Would you like to go out to eat tonight

10. The visit to the zoo was so much fun

11. I liked the exhibits at the art museum

12. Suzy wants to go on the riverboat

13. Isn't it great that Grandma and Grandpa can go with us

14. I hope you packed a swimming suit so we can go to the beach

15. I'm so excited that the carnival is in town

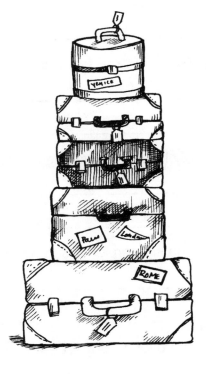

On Your Own: With a partner, write a silly story that contains all four types of sentences, but do not include the punctuation. Cut the sentences apart and put them in an envelope. Give them to another set of partners and have them arrange each sentence in the order they think it belongs. Then tell them to add the proper punctuation.

Name: _____ Date: _____

Unit 7: Punctuation—*The Period*

Key Ideas
- **The period** signals a full stop.
- Put a **period** after most abbreviations: Mr. Wifflestop, Mrs. Hoskins, Pres. Bush
- Put a **period** *inside* quotation marks.

Practice

Directions: Rewrite each sentence, adding the correct punctuation.

1. My brother said, "I work for Dr Who at the FBI"

   _____

   _____

2. Gen Robert E Lee led the Confederate Army during the Civil War

   _____

   _____

3. My little sister watches Sesame St almost every day during the summer

   _____

   _____

4. The sign on Marwood Ave said, "Stay Out"

   _____

   _____

5. The pilot, Bobby L Lewis, makes traffic reports on station WZZK

   _____

   _____

On Your Own: Make up a sentence that contains two abbreviations, a quotation, and ends in a period. Leave out the punctuation. Give it to a friend to see if he or she can punctuate the sentence correctly.

Name: _____ Date: _____

Unit 7: Punctuation—*The Comma*

Key Ideas

- The **comma** tells the reader to pause.

    Example: What do you think, should we go to the store or not?

- Use a **comma** to separate things in a list or series.

    Example: Next to the woman was a bassoon, a baboon, and a balloon.

- Use a **comma** to set off words or phrases that interrupt the sentence.

    Example: Now, let's get cracking!

- Use a **comma** to set off an appositive. An **appositive** is a noun or pronoun that explains or introduces the noun that comes before it.

    Example: Miss Milarke, my favorite teacher, just won a marathon.

- Put a **comma** *inside* quotation marks.

    Example: "Yes, I'm going to the mall," said Hannah, "to finish Christmas shopping."

Practice

Directions: Read the following sentences. Decide where commas should go and put them in using the editor's mark (⩕) for inserting a comma.

President for a Day

Lana the president of the student council was absent from school so I had to fill in for her. I had to call the meeting make the announcements record the minutes and conduct the business. Many students were fooling around. "Let's get down to business" I said. Paul asked if I had heard the rumors about the new lunch program. I told him "Yes I had heard the news." After much discussion we decided to meet again on Monday November 5 2001. With all my duties as temporary president I was tired and very glad the meeting was over!

On Your Own: Write a message to your mother or father telling her or him all the things you would like for your birthday. Be sure to write items in a series and not in a list. Use commas to set off the items in the series. Add the date to your message, and be sure to use commas correctly.

Name: _____ Date: _____

Unit 7: Punctuation—*Quotation Marks*

Key Idea
- Put **quotation marks** around the exact words of the speaker.

    Example: "Don't do it!" he shouted to the man.

Practice

Directions: Rewrite each of these sentences, adding the correct punctuation. Remember that periods and commas go inside the quotation marks. Remember also to capitalize the first word of each quotation.

1. Janet said I am going to the Philippine Islands on October 11 2001

   _____

   _____

2. What are you going to do there asked Ruby Jewell

   _____

   _____

3. Well she said I am going to work play and shop

   _____

   _____

4. Do people in the Philippine Islands speak english thomas asked

   _____

   _____

5. Some do some don't Janet replied

   _____

   _____

On Your Own: Make up a conversation between two or more people about an imaginary visit to someone in another country. Write out your conversation using some real facts about your location. Be sure to punctuate your conversation correctly.

Name: _____ Date: _____

Unit 7: Punctuation—*The Apostrophe*

Key Ideas

- An **apostrophe** is used to show ownership and means the noun *belongs to everything to the left of the apostrophe.*

    Example: The woman's fingernails were three inches long!

    woman's   =   the fingernails belong to the woman

- If the noun is plural and ends in "s," simply add the **apostrophe.**

    Example: The clowns' tricks made us laugh.

    clowns'   =   the tricks belong to the clowns

- If the word is a proper noun and ends in "s," add an **apostrophe** and an "s."

    Example: Ross's riddle stumped the class.

    Ross's   =   the riddle belongs to Ross

Practice

Directions: Use editor's marks: (⌄) and (⌄ⁱˢ) to indicate where apostrophes and apostrophe "s" go in this paragraph.

The Circus

The circus came to Yeats School last week. Yeats circus was the greatest show on Earth. The clowns tricks kept everyone laughing, especially when one clowns flower squirted water on the principal. The  crowd applause was loudest for the elephants dance and the acrobats skill. The boys cheers were the loudest for the lion tamers courage, but the lion fierce roar scared them. The ringmasters jokes were a big hit, and the performers costumes were admired by all. Yeats circus was a great success!

On Your Own: Write a personal narrative about an event that your school sponsored. Use as many ownership nouns and pronouns as you can to show your expertise in using apostrophes.

Name: _____ Date: _____

Unit 7: Punctuation Test

Directions: Read each sentence. Darken the circle next to the choice of the correctly punctuated word or group of words that will fill in the blank.

1. Eliza comes from _____.
   - ○ A. San, Francisco, California
   - ○ B. San, Francisco California
   - ○ C. San Francisco California
   - ○ D. San Francisco, California

2. The correct abbreviation for the word February is _____.
   - ○ A. Feb
   - ○ B. Feb.
   - ○ C. Feb;
   - ○ D. Feb,

3. _____ I heard you.
   - ○ A. Yes
   - ○ B. Yes;
   - ○ C. Yes,
   - ○ D. "Yes"

4. Our teacher said, _____
   - ○ A. "Please do not run."
   - ○ B. Please do not run.
   - ○ C. "Please do not run.
   - ○ D. Please do not run."

5. The correct way to write the date is _____.
   - ○ A. Saturday, March, 17, 2001
   - ○ B. Saturday March 17 2001
   - ○ C. Saturday, March 17 2001
   - ○ D. Saturday, March 17, 2001

6. Alarmed, the teacher called, "Stop running in the _____
   - ○ A. hallway.
   - ○ B. hallway!"
   - ○ C. hallway?
   - ○ D. hallway,

7. Is your bicycle _____
   - ○ A. broken.
   - ○ B. broken!
   - ○ C. broken?
   - ○ D. broken,

Name: _____ Date: _____

Unit 7: Punctuation Test (cont.)

8. She collects _____
   ○ A. stamps coins and postcards.
   ○ B. stamps, coins and postcards.
   ○ C. stamps, coins, and postcards.
   ○ D. stamps, coins, and, postcards.

9. _____ you still on the phone?
   ○ A. Mario are
   ○ B. Mario, are
   ○ C. Mario; are
   ○ D. "Mario" are

10. _____ team won the track meet!
   ○ A. Hurray our
   ○ B. Hurray, Our
   ○ C. Hurray our,
   ○ D. Hurray, our

11. Some of my favorite books are by _____.
   ○ A. E B White
   ○ B. E B. White
   ○ C. E. B. White
   ○ D. E, B. White

12. I think that is _____ blue jacket.
   ○ A. Katies
   ○ B. Katies'
   ○ C. Katie's
   ○ D. Katies's

13. We are going to a baseball game on _____.
   ○ A. Sunday July 15, 2001
   ○ B. Sunday, July 15, 2001
   ○ C. Sunday July 15 2001
   ○ D. Sunday, July 15 2001

14. "Your answer to question number four is incorrect _____.
   ○ A. , said Mr. Martinez
   ○ B. ." said Mr. Martinez
   ○ C. said Mr. Martinez
   ○ D. ," said Mr. Martinez

15. Abby _____ is also an honor student.
   ○ A. , our class president,
   ○ B. our class president,
   ○ C. , our class president
   ○ D. , our class president;

Name: _____ Date: _____

Unit 8: Usage—*Sentence Fragments*

Key Ideas
- A **sentence** is a group of words that states a *complete* thought.
  Example: The hobby of bird-watching is fascinating.

- A **sentence** has both a subject and a predicate.

  Example: subject   =   The hobby of bird-watching
  predicate   =   is fascinating.

- A **fragment** is an *incomplete* thought; it is missing either the subject or the predicate.
  Example: The hobby of bird-watching   (missing the predicate)
  is fascinating   (missing the subject)

Practice

Directions: Read each group of words. If it is a sentence, write "sentence" on the line; if it is missing either a subject or a predicate, write "fragment."

1. Because there are so many species. _____

2. Have many interesting behaviors. _____

3. Each kind of bird's nest is unique. _____

4. Many different materials. _____

5. City birds use twine, tin foil, paper, and
   tissue to build their nests. _____

6. An eagle's nest can weigh two tons. _____

7. Elaborate, woven nests of orioles. _____

8. Birds shed their old, worn-out feathers. _____

9. This is called molting. _____

10. Are important for a bird's survival. _____

11. Migration is an instinctive behavior for birds. _____

12. By nearly half the species of birds. _____

13. Some birds don't migrate. _____

14. The changing seasons. _____

15. Affect a bird's habitat. _____

On Your Own: Imagine you are a famous bird-watcher. Using the information above, write a story about your discovery of a new species of bird. Check to be sure there are not any sentence fragments.

Name: _____ Date: _____

Unit 8: Usage—*Run-on Sentences*

Key Ideas

- A **sentence** is a group of words that states a *complete* thought.

  Example: George Washington was our nation's first president.

- A **sentence** that has *two complete* thoughts or ideas with no punctuation is **a run-on sentence**.

  Example: George Washington was our nation's first president he was considered an honest man and a great general.

- A **run-on sentence** can be corrected by separating the *two complete* thoughts into *two complete* sentences.

  Example: George Washington was our nation's first president. He was considered an honest man and a great general.

Practice

Directions: On your own paper, rewrite each run-on sentence correctly, separating the two complete thoughts into two complete sentences.

1. George Washington was commander in chief of the Continental Army he was a great horseman.

2. George Washington married Martha Custis she was a widow with two children.

3. While a young man, he spent a lot of time outdoors he also enjoyed dancing.

4. The White House did not exist while Washington was president John Adams was the first president to live there.

5. George Washington inherited the plantation, Mount Vernon, it is located in Virginia.

6. He created a medal to recognize merit in the military it was called the Purple Heart.

7. While her husband was president, Martha's formal title was not Mrs. Washington she was addressed as Lady Washington.

8. There are many myths about Washington many of these were written about in two books by Parson Mason Weems.

9. One of the most popular myths was about George chopping down a cherry tree he confessed to his father.

10. Washington served eight years as president he retired to Mount Vernon.

On Your Own: Discover other famous "true stories" that are not true like the one about Washington and the cherry tree. Write an informational paragraph about one of them. Be sure to eliminate sentence fragments and run-on sentences from your paragraph.

Name: _____ Date: _____

Unit 8: Usage—*Simple and Compound Sentences*

Key Ideas

- A **simple sentence** contains *one* subject and *one* predicate.

    Example: The prisoners escaped.

subject	=	prisoners
predicate	=	escaped

- A **compound sentence** has *two or more* subject/predicate combinations.

    Example: You may want to go to Walt Disney World, or you may want to go to Treasure Island.

- **Combine** two simple sentences into a compound sentence to make your writing more interesting.

    Example: I got home. I took a nap.

                 After I got home, I took a nap.

Practice

Directions: On your own paper, rewrite each sentence by combining the two simple sentences into one compound sentence.

1. The workers at the school were told to put their oily rags in cans. They forgot to do it.

2. During the night, the rags caught fire. The fire spread quickly through the storeroom.

3. The smoke detector blared loudly. No one heard it.

4. A neighbor called 911. She saw flames shooting out of the windows.

5. Firefighters raced to the school. Smoke was pouring out of a hole in the roof.

6. Glass cracked from the heat of the fire. It shattered all over the sidewalk.

7. The firefighters needed more help. The captain called in another company.

8. Finally, the fire was brought under control. It took almost four hours to put it out.

9. Luckily, school was closed for summer vacation. No one was there at the time.

10. It's going to take about a month to clean and fix up the building. It is a real mess.

On Your Own: Rewrite these sentences as a news article. Be sure to answer *Who, What, When, Where, Why,* and *How.* Use as many compound sentences as you can in your news article.

Name: _____ Date: _____

Unit 8: Usage—*Precise Words*

Key Idea
- Use **precise words** to make your writing clearer, more interesting, and easier to understand.

    Example: Joann reads <u>books</u> to her little sister.

    Replace the word "books" with more precise words, such as "fairy tales."
    Joann reads <u>fairy tales</u> to her little sister.

Practice

Directions: Replace each underlined word with a more precise word from the word bank, and write it on the lines below. Be sure the word fits the meaning of the sentence.

dog	roses	angry	repair	grinned	destruction
canine	enjoys	vibrant	garden	damage	embarrassed
confine	sometimes	apologize	poppies	escape	obedient
mischief	teach	behave	sensible		

1. My <u>pet</u> dug up my cousin's <u>flowers</u>.

   _____

2. My cousin was very <u>mad</u> about the <u>mess</u> in her favorite <u>spot</u>.

   _____

3. I felt <u>funny</u> about the <u>thing</u> my dog did.

   _____

4. I tried to <u>say sorry</u> for what he did by bringing her some <u>bright</u> red <u>flowers</u>.

   _____

5. She <u>smiled</u> and said she wasn't irritated with me but with my <u>dog</u>.

   _____

6. It would be <u>wise</u> to <u>keep</u> him in the yard.

   _____

7. I hope he doesn't <u>get out</u> again and cause any more <u>trouble</u>.

   _____

8. He is usually <u>good</u>, but <u>once in a while</u> he can be bad.

   _____

9. Maybe I should try to <u>show</u> him how to <u>be good</u>.

   _____

10. My cousin really <u>likes</u> gardening, and she will <u>fix</u> the damage in no time.

    _____

On Your Own: Take one of your recent journal entries and identify at least five words that you can replace with more precise words to make your writing more colorful and interesting.

Name: _____ Date: _____

Unit 8: Usage—*Verbs That Agree*

Key Idea
- Singular subjects take singular **verbs**, and plural subjects take plural **verbs**.

   Example: Wearing a red hat and yellow socks, Bob was sitting in the box-seat section of the ballpark.

   subject   =   Bob (singular)
   verb   =   was sitting (singular)

Practice

Directions: Circle the correct verb in each of the following sentences.

1. My neighbor's nose (was, were) frostbitten.

2. Frostbitten ears (is, are) very painful.

3. We (was, were) glad to get warm.

4. Susan, wearing thick gloves, (is, are) warm and toasty.

5. Many of the causes of frostbite (is, are) known and can be prevented.

6. The danger of frostbitten toes (do, does) worry my neighbor's son.

7. Neither Lateesha nor Rick (desire, desires) a frostbitten nose.

8. Lizzy, together with Diana, (want, wants) to avoid frostbite when they hike.

9. Meredith's family (is, are) wondering whether there (is, are) anything they can do to

   prevent Meredith from getting frostbitten when she climbs the mountain.

10. Everyone who (comes, come) to visit (see, sees) that extra

   socks (prevents, prevent) frostbite on toes.

On Your Own: Write an individual or collaborative report on the causes of frostbite. Make sure your verbs agree in number with your subjects.

Unit 8: Usage—"How Many?" Adjectives

Key Ideas

- **Adjectives** are words that describe nouns and pronouns.

  Example: Billy is a black horse with a beautiful, flowing mane.

  Adjectives = beautiful, flowing

- **Adjectives** that describe how much or how many are often misused. If you are talking about something that can be counted individually, use *fewer, many,* or *number.*

  If you are talking about something that can't be counted individually—something that is more like a group or a bunch—use *less, amount,* or *much.*

  Example: Lucy ate <u>fewer</u> potato chips than Zeb did.
  Dixon ate <u>less</u> mashed potatoes than I did.

Practice

Directions: Circle the correct adjective in each sentence.

1. Last night I ate (fewer, less) cookies than my sister Carol.

2. Although Carol ate (many, more) cookies than I, she ate (fewer, less) pudding.

3. We took (fewer, less) free samples than was expected.

4. The (number, amount) of people who came to see the movie was overwhelming.

5. (Fewer, Less) popcorn was sold than the owners anticipated.

6. The (amount, number) of sodas that was sold surprised them.

7. Joyce helped herself to (much, many) of the sponge cake.

8. The (number, amount) of students absent from school was surprising.

9. How (much, many) campers are coming this week?

10. The happy clown performed (fewer, less) tricks than the sad clown.

11. Although she already had two, Jenna needed (many, more) sweaters for her ski trip.

12. At the children's lemonade stand, they sold (fewer, less) glasses today than yesterday.

13. The weatherman predicted (much, many) days of rain this spring.

14. The (amount, number) of cars at the car wash was (many, more) than last year.

15. The price for the cruise was (fewer, less) money than my parents thought.

On Your Own: Write a news bulletin that uses correctly the adjectives: *less, more, fewer, much, many, number,* and *amount.* When you are ready, share with a friend.

Name: _____ Date: _____

Unit 8: Usage—*Pronouns and Their Homophones*

Key Idea

- Do not confuse the contractions *it's, they're,* and *you're* with their homophones *its, their, there,* and *your.*

it's	=	it is		you're	=	you are
its	=	belonging to it		your	=	belonging to you
they're	=	they are		their	=	belonging to them
there	=	in a place				

Practice

Directions: This report has six incorrect pronouns. Underline the pronoun errors and write the correct word above the error.

Poison Frogs

Everyone has seen a frog. Their a familiar sight around marshes and ponds. Their is another kind of frog, however, that is very poisonous. Only a tiny pinprick of it's skin secretion is enough to kill a human being. If your in South or Central America, look out for this black and yellow frog. Its the kind of frog you don't want in you're suitcase.

Directions: Circle the correct pronoun in each sentence.

1. Last night I saw (there, their) dog running up the street.

2. Cassie's brother will help you with (you're, your) homework, even though (it's, its) late.

3. How many students were (their, there) at the football game?

4. (Their, They're) the only people in the neighborhood who have a swimming pool.

5. Did you know that a snake sheds (its, it's) skin?

On Your Own: Write your own nature report about an unusual animal or amphibian. Use the homophones from above in your report. Read your report aloud. Ask your classmates how to spell each homophone.

Name: _____ Date: _____

Unit 8: Usage—*"Good" Adjectives and "Well" Adverbs*

Key Ideas

- **Adjectives** describe nouns and pronouns.

- **Adverbs** describe verbs, adjectives, or other adverbs and tell where, when, or how.

     Example: Mr. Richards is a *good* tour guide because he speaks *well*.
          good   =   adjective, describes tour guide (noun)
          well   =   adverb, describes speaks (verb)

Practice

Directions: Use *good* or *well* to complete each sentence correctly.

1. The donuts we made this morning were _____.

2. We mixed and fried the dough _____.

3. Rebecca didn't decorate them very _____, however.

4. She didn't sleep _____ last night and was very tired.

5. Erika decided that Rebecca hadn't made a very _____ decision to come to work.

6. Rebecca just didn't feel _____, so we sent her home to rest.

7. The rest of the morning in the bakery went _____.

8. There were several _____ orders for donuts placed by businesses.

9. Erika and Maggie filled in for Rebecca and did a _____ job decorating cakes and cookies.

10. A lady came in and asked me what would be a _____ character to put on her toddler's birthday cake.

11. A man asked what colors would go _____ with hot pink and orange.

12. I don't think anything looks _____ with that combination of colors!

13. That wouldn't have been a _____ thing to tell him, however.

14. I'm glad that everyone else was feeling _____; it was a busy day.

15. It will be _____ to finish up and relax after a hard day's work.

On Your Own: Write a brief review of your favorite movie. Use the words *good* and *well*. Then copy your review leaving a blank where you used *good* or *well*. Give it to a friend and have him or her fill in the blanks with the correct words. Check to see if he or she is correct.

Name: _____ Date: _____

Unit 8: Usage Test

Directions: Read each sentence. Darken the circle next to the best answer.

1. Which one of the following is *not* correct?
   - ○ A. My brother, John. Is in first grade.
   - ○ B. My brother John is in first grade.
   - ○ C. My brother John is seven and in first grade.

2. Which one of the following is *not* correct?
   - ○ A. I could lose weight if I ran home every day.
   - ○ B. I could lose weight. if I ran home every day.
   - ○ C. If I ran home every day, I could lose weight.

3. Which one of the following is *not* correct?
   - ○ A. Although Wanda loves chocolate, she rarely eats it.
   - ○ B. Wanda rarely eats chocolate although she loves it.
   - ○ C. Although Wanda loves chocolate. She rarely eats it.

4. Which of the following sentences contains a *run-on* sentence?
   - ○ A. Because the weather is so beautiful today, we are going on a picnic.
   - ○ B. We are going on a picnic because the weather is so beautiful today.
   - ○ C. The weather is so beautiful today we are going on a picnic.

5. Which of the following sentences contains a *run-on* sentence?
   - ○ A. When Erica played in the basketball game, she injured her knee.
   - ○ B. Erica played in the basketball game she injured her knee.
   - ○ C. Erica injured her knee when she played in the basketball game.

6. Which of these sentences contains the most <u>precise</u> use of words?
   - ○ A. Liz is *smart.*
   - ○ B. Liz is *intelligent.*

7. Which of these sentences contains the most <u>precise</u> use of words?
   - ○ A. The boys *carried* water buckets out to the men in the field.
   - ○ B. The boys *hauled* water buckets out to the men in the field.

8. Which of these sentences is correct?
   - ○ A. The village have a fair today.
   - ○ B. The village has a fair today.

Name: _____ Date: _____

Unit 8: Usage Test (cont.)

9. Which of these sentences is correct?
   ○ A. Ronnie and Johnny have a float entered in the parade.
   ○ B. Ronnie and Johnny has a float entered in the parade.

10. Which of these sentences is correct?
    ○ A. Sam, together with Lisa, want to win the contest.
    ○ B. Sam, together with Lisa, wants to win the contest.

11. Which of these sentences is correct?
    ○ A. At the bake sale, we received fewer cakes, but many cookies.
    ○ B. At the bake sale, we received less cakes, but much cookies.

12. Which of these sentences is correct?
    ○ A. There are many strangers in the village today.
    ○ B. Their are many strangers in the village today.
    ○ C. They're many strangers in the village today.

13. Which of these sentences is correct?
    ○ A. If you eat all that junk food, your going to be sorry.
    ○ B. If you eat all that junk food, you're going to be sorry.

14. Which of these sentences is correct?
    ○ A. Red goes well with green.
    ○ B. Red goes good with green.

15. Which of these sentences is correct?
    ○ A. Darian went home because he didn't feel good.
    ○ B. Darian went home because he didn't feel well.

Section III: Putting It All Together—*Introduction*

Now that you've practiced and applied the writing process, forms of writing, and the conventions of writing, it is time to **put it all together**. Included in this section are writing rubrics for teachers and students, student writing prompts, and a writing skills test.

Teacher Evaluation Rubrics - The rubrics for evaluating student writing have been designed to be developmental. The scoring grid ranges from *"not yet"* to *"strong"* competency and can show a writer's developmental progress over time. It is intended that teachers and students focus on one characteristic at a time, building up to the use of the comprehensive evaluation rubric. The writing rubrics cover the following characteristics that are important to teachers and other evaluators:

- **Ideas/Content:** The content is focused, original, and interesting.
- **Organization:** The organization is clear and helpful to the reader.
- **Voice:** The writer's voice is lively and interesting.
- **Word Choice:** The writer uses rich, colorful language.
- **Sentence Fluency:** The flow and rhythm of the writing aid in reading the piece aloud.
- **Conventions:** The mechanics and correctness of the writing are strong.

- **Evaluation Rubric:** This rubric covers all the above characteristics and is intended for use *after* the characteristics have been explored and developed.

Student Self-Evaluation Rubrics - The self-evaluation rubrics consist of lists of questions for the writer to ask himself/herself about the writing. They are intended to focus the writer's attention on the characteristics being studied (i.e., on the teacher rubrics). They are more informal than the teacher evaluation rubrics and are intended to be used during the final editing stage of writing. Like the teacher rubrics, there are self-evaluation rubrics for **Ideas/Content**, **Organization**, **Voice**, **Word Choice**, **Sentence Fluency**, and **Conventions/Presentation**. Finally, there is a comprehensive **Self-Evaluation Student Rubric** included.

Student Peer Evaluation Rubric - This rubric is designed for students to use when evaluating the writing of their peers. It can be used during the revising and editing stages of writing. It is a comprehensive rubric that covers all the characteristics listed above.

Student Writing Prompts - The purpose of the writing prompts is to apply, *in a testing situation,* the knowledge and skills students gain from the practice activities.

Name: _____ Date: _____

Topic: _____

Type of Writing: _____

Teacher Scoring Rubric for Evaluating Student Writing

Directions: Circle the number that best describes the quality of the writing.

1 **Not Yet:** A bare beginning; writer not yet showing any control
2 **Emerging:** Need for revision outweighs strengths; isolated moments hint at what the writer has in mind
3 **Developing:** Strengths and need for revision are about equal; about halfway home
4 **Effective:** On balance, the strengths outweigh the weaknesses; a small amount of revision is needed
5 **Strong:** Shows control and skill in this trait; many strengths present
6 **Wow!** Exceeds expectations

Features	Not Yet	Emerging	Developing	Effective	Strong
Ideas: The paper is clear and focused; it holds the reader's attention; relevant anecdotes and details enrich the central theme.	1	2	3	4	5
Organization: The organization enhances and showcases the central idea or theme. The order and structure of information is compelling and moves the reader through the text.	1	2	3	4	5
Voice: The writer speaks directly to the reader in a way that is individual, compelling, and engaging. The writer crafts the writing with an awareness and respect for the audience and the purpose for writing.	1	2	3	4	5
Word Choice: Words convey the intended message in a precise, interesting, and natural way. The words are powerful and engaging.	1	2	3	4	5
Sentence Fluency: The writing has an easy flow, rhythm, and cadence. Sentences are well built, with strong and varied structure that invites expressive oral reading.	1	2	3	4	5
Conventions: The writer demonstrates a good and age-appropriate grasp of standard writing conventions—spelling, punctuation, capitalization, grammar, usage, and paragraphing.	1	2	3	4	5
Presentation: The form and presentation of the text enhance the reader's ability to understand and connect with the message. The piece is pleasing to the eye.	1	2	3	4	5

Comments: _____

Name: _____ Date: _____

Topic: _____

Type of Writing: _____

1. Scoring Rubric for Evaluating Ideas

Directions: Circle the number that best describes the quality of the writing.

1 **Not Yet:** A bare beginning; writer not yet showing any control
2 **Emerging:** Need for revision outweighs strengths; isolated moments hint at what the writer has in mind
3 **Developing:** Strengths and need for revision are about equal; about halfway home
4 **Effective:** On balance, the strengths outweigh the weaknesses; a small amount of revision is needed
5 **Strong:** Shows control and skill in this trait; many strengths present
6 **Wow!** Exceeds expectations

Features	Not Yet	Emerging	Developing	Effective	Strong
Ideas:	1	2	3	4	5

	Not Yet (1)	Emerging (2-3)		Strong (4-5)

This paper has no clear sense of purpose or central theme. To extract meaning from the text, the reader must make inferences based on sketchy or missing details. The writing reflects more than one of these problems.
*The writer is still in search of a topic, brainstorming, or has not yet decided what the main idea of the piece will be.
*Information is limited or unclear, or the length is not adequate for development.
*The idea is a simple restatement of the topic or an answer to the question with little or no attention to detail.
*The writer has not begun to define the topic in a meaningful, personal way.
*Everything seems as important as everything else; the reader has a hard time sifting out what is important.
*The text may be repetitious, or it may read like a collection of disconnected, random thoughts with no discernible point.

This writer is beginning to define the topic, even though development is still basic or general.
*The topic is fairly broad; however, you can see where the writer is headed.
*Support is attempted, but doesn't go far enough yet in fleshing out the key issues or story line.
*Ideas are reasonably clear, though they may not be detailed, personalized, accurate, or expanded enough to show in-depth understanding or a strong sense of purpose.
*The writer seems to be drawing on knowledge or experience but has difficulty going from general observations to specifics.
*The reader is left with questions. More information is needed to fill in the blanks.
*The writer generally stays on the topic but does not develop a clear theme. The writer has not yet focused the topic past the obvious.

This paper is clear and focused. It holds the reader's attention. Relevant anecdotes and details enrich the central theme.
*The topic is narrow and manageable.
*Relevant, telling, quality details give the reader important information that goes beyond the obvious or predictable.
*Reasonably accurate details are present to support the main ideas.
*The writer seems to be writing from knowledge or experience; the ideas are fresh and original.
*The reader's questions are anticipated and answered.
*Insight—an understanding of life and a knack for picking out what is significant—is the indicator of high-level performance, though not required.

Comments: _____

Name: _____ Date: _____

Topic: _____

Type of Writing: _____

2. Scoring Rubric for Evaluating Organization

Directions: Circle the number that best describes the quality of the writing.

1 **Not Yet:**   A bare beginning; writer not yet showing any control
2 **Emerging:**   Need for revision outweighs strengths; isolated moments hint at what the writer has in mind
3 **Developing:**   Strengths and need for revision are about equal; about halfway home
4 **Effective:**   On balance, the strengths outweigh the weaknesses; a small amount of revision is needed
5 **Strong:**   Shows control and skill in this trait; many strengths present
6 **Wow!**   Exceeds expectations

Features	Not Yet	Emerging	Developing	Effective	Strong
Organization:	1	2	3	4	5
	The writing lacks a clear sense of direction. Ideas, details, or events seem strung together in a loose or random fashion; there is no identifiable internal structure. The writing reflects more than one of these problems: *There is no real lead to set up what follows, no real conclusion to wrap things up. *Connections between ideas are confusing or not even present. *Sequencing needs lots and lots of work. *Pacing feels awkward; the writer slows to a crawl when the reader wants to get on with it, and vice versa. *No title is present (if requested) or, if present, does not match well with the content. *Problems with organization make it hard for the reader to get a grip on the main point or story line.		The organizational structure is strong enough to move the reader through the text without too much confusion. *The paper has a recognizable introduction and conclusion. The introduction may not create a strong sense of anticipation; the conclusion may not tie up all loose ends. *Transitions often work well; at other times, connections between ideas are fuzzy. *Sequencing shows some logic, but is not under control enough that it consistently supports the ideas. In fact, sometimes the sequencing is so predictable and rehearsed that it takes attention away from the content. *Pacing is fairly well controlled, though the writer sometimes lunges ahead too quickly or spends too much time on details that do not matter. *A title (if desired) is present, although it may be uninspired or an obvious restatement of the prompt or topic. *The organization sometimes supports the main point or story line; at other times, the reader feels an urge to add a transition or move things around.		The organization enhances and showcases the central idea or theme. The order and structure of information is compelling and moves the reader through the text. *An inviting introduction draws the reader in; a satisfying conclusion leaves the reader with a sense of closure and resolution. *Thoughtful transitions clearly show how ideas connect. *Details seem to fit where they're placed; sequencing is logical and effective. *Pacing is well controlled; the writer knows when to slow down and elaborate and when to pick up the pace and move on. *The title, if desired, is original and captures the central theme of the piece. *Organization flows so smoothly the reader hardly thinks about it; the choice of structure matches the purpose and audience.

Comments: _____

_____

Name: _____ Date: _____

Topic: _____

Type of Writing: _____

3. Scoring Rubric for Evaluating Voice

Directions: Circle the number that best describes the quality of the writing.

1 **Not Yet:**   A bare beginning; writer not yet showing any control
2 **Emerging:**   Need for revision outweighs strengths; isolated moments hint at what the writer has in mind
3 **Developing:** Strengths and need for revision are about equal; about halfway home
4 **Effective:**   On balance, the strengths outweigh the weaknesses; a small amount of revision is needed
5 **Strong:**   Shows control and skill in this trait; many strengths present
6 **Wow!**   Exceeds expectations

Features	Not Yet	Emerging	Developing	Effective	Strong
Voice:	**1**	**2**	**3**	**4**	**5**
	The writer seems indifferent, uninvolved, or distanced from the topic and/or the audience. As a result, the paper reflects more than one of the following problems: *The writer is not concerned with the audience. The writer's style is a complete mismatch for the intended reader or the writing is so short that little is accomplished beyond introducing the topic. *The writer speaks in a kind of monotone that flattens all potential highs or lows of the message. *The writing is humdrum and "risk-free." *The writing is lifeless or mechanical; depending on the topic, it may be overly technical or jargonistic. *The development of the topic is so limited that no point of view is present.		The writer seems sincere but not fully engaged or involved. The result is pleasant or even personable, but not compelling. *The writer seems aware of an audience but discards personal insights in favor of obvious generalities. *The writing communicates in an earnest, pleasing, yet safe manner. *Only one or two moments here or there intrigue, delight, or move the reader. These places may emerge strongly for a line or two, but quickly fade away. *Expository or persuasive writing lacks consistent engagement with the topic to build credibility. *Narrative writing is reasonably sincere, but doesn't reflect a unique or individual perspective about the topic.		The writer speaks directly to the reader in a way that is individual, compelling, and engaging. The writer crafts the writing with an awareness and respect for the audience and the purpose for writing. *The tone of the writing adds interest to the message and is appropriate for the purpose and audience. *The reader feels a strong interaction with the writer, sensing the person behind the words. *The writer takes a risk by revealing who he or she is consistently throughout the piece. *Expository or persuasive writing reflects a strong commitment to the topic by showing why the reader needs to know this and why he or she should care. *Narrative writing is honest, personal, and engaging, and makes you think about and react to the author's ideas and point of view.

Comments: _____

_____

Used with permission from the Northwest Regional Educational Laboratory (NWREL).

Name: _____ Date: _____

Topic: _____

Type of Writing: _____

4. Scoring Rubric for Evaluating Word Choice

Directions: Circle the number that best describes the quality of the writing.

1 **Not Yet:**   A bare beginning; writer not yet showing any control
2 **Emerging:**   Need for revision outweighs strengths; isolated moments hint at what the writer has in mind
3 **Developing:**   Strengths and need for revision are about equal; about halfway home
4 **Effective:**   On balance, the strengths outweigh the weaknesses; a small amount of revision is needed
5 **Strong:**   Shows control and skill in this trait; many strengths present
6 **Wow!**   Exceeds expectations

Features	Not Yet	Emerging	Developing	Effective	Strong
Word Choice:	1	2	3	4	5
	The writer demonstrates a limited vocabulary or has not searched for words to convey specific meaning. *Words are so nonspecific and distracting that only a very limited meaning comes through. *Problems with language leave the reader wondering. Many of the words just don't work in this piece. *Audience has not been considered. Language is used incorrectly, making the message secondary to the misfires with the words. *Limited vocabulary and/or misused parts of speech seriously impair understanding. *Words and phrases are so unimaginative and lifeless that they detract from the meaning. *Jargon or clichés distract or mislead. Redundancy may distract the reader.		**The language is functional, even if it lacks much energy. It is easy to figure out the writer's meaning on a general level.** *Words are adequate and correct in a general sense, and they support the meaning by not getting in the way. *Familiar words and phrases communicate but rarely capture the reader's imagination. *Attempts at colorful language show a willingness to stretch and grow but sometimes reach beyond the audience (thesaurus overload!). *Despite a few successes, the writing is marked by passive verbs, everyday nouns, and mundane modifiers. *The words and phrases are functional with only one or two fine moments. *The words may be refined in a couple of places, but the language looks more like the first thing that popped into the writer's mind.		**Words are powerful and engaging, and convey the intended message in a precise, interesting, and natural way.** *Words are specific and accurate. It is easy to understand just what the writer means. *Striking words and phrases often catch the reader's eye and linger in the reader's mind. *Language and phrasing are natural, effective, and appropriate for the audience. *Lively verbs add energy, while specific nouns and modifiers add depth. *Choices in language enhance the meaning and clarify understanding. *Precision is obvious. The writer has taken care to put just the right word or phrase in just the right spot.

Comments: _____

_____

Name: _____ Date: _____

Topic: _____

Type of Writing: _____

5. Scoring Rubric for Evaluating Sentence Fluency

Directions: Circle the number that best describes the quality of the writing.

1 **Not Yet:**   A bare beginning; writer not yet showing any control
2 **Emerging:**   Need for revision outweighs strengths; isolated moments hint at what the writer has in mind
3 **Developing:** Strengths and need for revision are about equal; about halfway home
4 **Effective:**   On balance, the strengths outweigh the weaknesses; a small amount of revision is needed
5 **Strong:**   Shows control and skill in this trait; many strengths present
6 **Wow!**   Exceeds expectations

Features	Not Yet	Emerging	Developing	Effective	Strong
Sentence Fluency:	1	2	3	4	5
	The reader has to practice quite a bit in order to give this paper a fair interpretive reading. The writing reflects more than one of the following problems: *Sentences are choppy, incomplete, rambling, or awkward; they need work. Phrasing does not sound natural. The patterns may create a singsong rhythm or a chop-chop cadence that lulls the reader to sleep. *There is little or no "sentence sense" present. Even if this piece were flawlessy edited, the sentences would not hang together. *Many sentences begin the same way—and may follow the same patterns (for example, *subject-verb-object*) in a monotonous pattern. *Endless connectives (*and, and so, but then, because, and then,* etc.) or a complete lack of connectives creates a massive jumble of language. *The text does not invite expressive oral reading.		The text hums along with a steady beat but tends to be more pleasant or businesslike than musical, more mechanical than fluid. *Although sentences may not seem artfully crafted or musical, they get the job done in a routine fashion. *Sentences are usually constructed correctly; they hang together; they are sound. *Sentence beginnings are not ALL alike; some variety is attempted. *The reader sometimes has to hunt for clues (for example, connecting words and phrases like *however, therefore, after a while, for example, next, later,* etc.) that show how sentences interrelate. *Parts of the text invite expressive oral reading; others may be stiff, awkward, choppy, or gangly.		The writing has an easy flow, rhythm, and cadence. Sentences are well built, with strong and varied structure that invites expressive oral reading. *Sentences are constructed in a way that underscores and enhances meaning. *Sentences vary in length as well as structure. Fragments, if used, add style. Dialogue, if present, sounds natural. *Purposeful and varied sentence beginnings add variety and energy. *The use of creative and appropriate connectives between sentences and thoughts shows how each relates to and builds upon the one before it. *The writing has cadence; the writer has thought about the sound of the words as well as the meaning. The first time you read it aloud is a breeze.

Comments: _____

Name: _____ Date: _____

Topic: _____

Type of Writing: _____

6. Scoring Rubric for Evaluating Conventions

Directions: Circle the number that best describes the quality of the writing.

1 **Not Yet:**   A bare beginning; writer not yet showing any control
2 **Emerging:**   Need for revision outweighs strengths; isolated moments hint at what the writer has in mind
3 **Developing:** Strengths and need for revision are about equal; about halfway home
4 **Effective:**   On balance, the strengths outweigh the weaknesses; a small amount of revision is needed
5 **Strong:**   Shows control and skill in this trait; many strengths present
6 **Wow!**   Exceeds expectations

Features	Not Yet	Emerging	Developing	Effective	Strong
Conventions:	1	2	3	4	5
	Errors in spelling, punctuation, capitalization, usage, grammar, and/or paragraphing repeatedly distract the reader and make the text difficult to read. The writing reflects more than one of these problems: *Spelling errors are frequent, even on common words. *Punctuation (including terminal punctuation) is often missing or incorrect. *Capitalization is random, and only the easiest rules show awareness of correct use. *Errors in grammar or usage are very noticeable and frequent and affect meaning. *Paragraphing is missing, irregular, or so frequent (every sentence) that it has no relationship to the organizational structure of the text. *The reader must read once to decode, then again for meaning. Extensive editing (virtually every line) would be required to polish the text for publication.		The writer shows reasonable control over a limited range of standard writing conventions. Conventions are sometimes handled well and enhance readability; at other times, errors are distracting and impair readability. *Spelling is usually correct or reasonably phonetic on common words, but more difficult words are problematic. *End punctuation is usually correct; internal punctuation *(commas, apostrophes, semicolons, dashes, colons, parentheses)* is sometimes missing/wrong. *Most words are capitalized correctly; control over more sophisticated capitalization skills may be spotty. *Problems with grammar or usage are not serious enough to distort meaning but may not be correct or accurately applied all of the time. *Paragraphing is attempted but may run together or begin in the wrong places. *Moderate editing (a little of this, a little of that) would be required to polish the text for publication.		The writer demonstrates a good grasp of standard writing conventions (spelling, punctuation, capitalization, grammar, usage, paragraphing) and uses conventions effectively to enhance readability. Errors tend to be so few that just minor touchups would get this piece ready to publish. *Spelling is generally correct, even on more difficult words. *The punctuation is accurate, even creative, and guides the reader through the text. *A thorough understanding and consistent application of capitalization skills are present. *Grammar and usage are correct and contribute to clarity and style. *Paragraphing tends to be sound and reinforces the organizational structure. *The writer may manipulate conventions for stylistic effect—and it works! The piece is very close to being ready to publish. *Writing shows control over those conventions that are grade/age appropriate.

Comments: _____
_____

Name: _____ Date: _____

Topic: _____

Type of Writing: _____

Student Scoring Rubric for Evaluating Peer Writing

Directions: Circle the number that best describes the quality of the writing.

1 **Not Yet:** A bare beginning; writer not yet showing any control
2 **Emerging:** Need for revision outweighs strengths; isolated moments hint at what the writer has in mind
3 **Developing:** Strengths and need for revision are about equal; about halfway home
4 **Effective:** On balance, the strengths outweigh the weaknesses; a small amount of revision is needed
5 **Strong:** Shows control and skill in this trait; many strengths present
6 **Wow!** Exceeds expectations

Features	Not Yet	Emerging	Developing	Effective	Strong
Ideas: Is the paper clear and focused? Does it hold the reader's attention?	1	2	3	4	5
Organization: Does the organization enhance the central idea and move the reader through the text?	1	2	3	4	5
Voice: Does the writer speak directly to the reader in a way that is individual, compelling, and engaging?	1	2	3	4	5
Word Choice: Do the words convey the intended message in a precise, interesting, and natural way? Are the words powerful and engaging?	1	2	3	4	5
Sentence Fluency: Does the writing have an easy flow, rhythm, and cadence? Are sentences well built, with strong and varied structure that invites expressive oral reading?	1	2	3	4	5
Conventions: Does the writer demonstrate a good grasp of spelling, punctuation, capitalization, grammar, usage, and paragraphing?	1	2	3	4	5
Presentation: Does the form and presentation of the paper enhance the reader's ability to understand and connect with the message? Is the piece pleasing to the eye?	1	2	3	4	5

Comments: _____

Name: _____ Date: _____

Student Evaluation: Writing Rubric

Topic: _____

Type of Writing: *Expository*   *Persuasive*   *Narrative*

Directions: Check those statements that apply to your piece of writing.

_____ I have a clear and interesting topic that I care about.

_____ My writing is based on my own experience or my own investigation into the topic.

_____ I can sum up my main point in one sentence: _____

_____

_____ I have a strong beginning that "grabs" my reader's attention.

_____ I have included all important events in the order of their happening.

_____ My writing is easy to follow; each point leads to the next point.

_____ I show things happening rather than *telling* about them.

_____ My writing has energy, enthusiasm, and confidence and sounds like me.

_____ My language is appropriate to my topic and audience.

_____ My story reads well out loud.

_____ My writing reaches out to "grab" my reader's attention and holds it right up to the end.

_____ I have a strong ending that leaves my reader satisfied.

_____ There are no significant errors in my paper.

_____ I revised and edited this paper carefully.

Comments: _____

_____

_____

_____

Name: _____ Date: _____

Student Evaluation: Writing Rubric—*Ideas*

Topic: _____

Type of Writing: *Expository*   *Persuasive*   *Narrative*

Directions: Check those statements that apply to your piece of writing.

_____   I have a clear and interesting topic that I care about.

_____   My writing is based on my own experience or my own investigation into the topic.

_____   I can sum up my main point in one sentence: _____

_____

_____   I have a strong beginning that "grabs" my reader's attention.

_____   All of my sentences are important to the topic.

_____   I have included all important events in the order of their happening.

_____   I show things happening rather than *telling* about them.

_____   I have a strong ending that leaves my reader satisfied.

_____   My readers aren't left with any important unanswered questions.

Comments: _____

_____

_____

_____

_____

_____

_____

_____

Student Evaluation: Writing Rubric—*Organization*

Name: _____ Date: _____

Student Evaluation: Writing Rubric—*Organization*

Topic: _____

Type of Writing: *Expository*   *Persuasive*   *Narrative*

Directions: Check those statements that apply to your piece of writing.

_____   I have a clear and interesting topic.

_____   I have a strong beginning that "grabs" my reader's attention.

_____   My writing is easy to follow. Each point leads to the next point.

_____   I have included all important events in the order of their happening.

_____   My details add to the story and make it more colorful and interesting.

_____   I show things happening rather than *telling* about them.

_____   I have included dialogue when appropriate.

_____   I have a strong ending that leaves my reader satisfied.

_____   My ending tells how the story worked out or how I felt about it.

_____   My readers aren't left with any important unanswered questions.

Comments: _____

_____

_____

_____

_____

_____

_____

_____

Name: _____ Date: _____

Student Evaluation: Writing Rubric—*Word Choice*

Topic: _____

Type of Writing:　　*Expository*　　　　*Persuasive*　　　　*Narrative*

Directions: Check those statements that apply to your piece of writing.

_____　　I have used many interesting words in my writing; I have used words that I *like.*

_____　　I chose just the right words to express my ideas and feelings.

_____　　I used phrases and words that are colorful and lively.

_____　　I chose words that help the reader see, feel, and understand my message.

_____　　I have used everyday words well and some everyday words in new and surprising ways.

_____　　My words show action, energy, and/or movement.

_____　　I used words that clearly convey feelings.

_____　　My story reads well out loud.

_____　　My readers will be clear about what my words mean.

Comments: _____

_____

_____

_____

_____

_____

_____

_____

Name: _____ Date: _____

Student Evaluation: Writing Rubric—*Sentence Fluency*

Topic: _____

Type of Writing: *Expository*   *Persuasive*   *Narrative*

Directions: Check those statements that apply to your piece of writing.

_____   My sentences are clear and varied.

_____   My paper has "rhythm" when read aloud; my writing is smooth.

_____   I have used different sentence beginnings; all of my sentences do not begin the same way.

_____   I have written some long sentences and some short sentences.

_____   Some of my sentences are simple, and some are complex.

_____   I used time clues when appropriate.

_____   Every sentence in my paper is a sentence: no run-on sentences or fragments.

_____   My sentences are concise, not wordy.

_____   My writing is easy for the reader to follow.

Comments: _____

_____

_____

_____

_____

_____

_____

Name: _____ Date: _____

Student Evaluation: Writing Rubric—*Conventions/Presentation*

Topic: _____

Type of Writing: *Expository*   *Persuasive*   *Narrative*

Directions: Check those statements that apply to your piece of writing.

_____   My spelling is correct.

_____   My punctuation is correct.

_____   My grammar is correct.

_____   I have carefully revised this paper.

_____   I have carefully edited this paper.

_____   There are no significant errors in my paper.

_____   My format is appropriate for my audience and for my purpose.

_____   Readers can read my handwriting.

_____   I have a "dy - no - mite" title for my paper.

Comments: _____

_____

_____

_____

_____

_____

_____

_____

Name: _____ Date: _____

Student Writing Sample With Teacher Prompt— *Personal Narrative*

Writing Situation: In this lesson you will write a personal narrative—a story that is true and that happened to you.

Trying new things can be scary. Write about a time you tried something new.

Directions for Writing: Before you begin writing, you will use scratch paper or the space below to brainstorm and organize your ideas. Use your imagination to make your writing colorful and interesting.

Use the best English you can, but do not worry about mistakes. The most important thing is to be clear so that the person reading your writing can imagine what your experience was like for you.

_____

_____

_____

_____

_____

_____

_____

_____

_____

_____

_____

_____

_____

_____

_____

Student Writing Sample With Teacher Prompt— *Informative Writing*

Writing Situation: In this lesson you will write about the power of being invisible.

Directions for Writing: Before you begin writing, use scratch paper or the space below to list all of the good and bad things you can think of about having this ability.

Use the best English you can, but do not worry about mistakes. The most important thing is to write clearly so your readers will understand what you are trying to say. Use the notes you made on the scratch paper to stay organized.

_____

_____

_____

_____

_____

_____

_____

_____

_____

_____

_____

_____

_____

_____

_____

_____

_____

_____

Name: _____ Date: _____

Student Writing Sample With Teacher Prompt— *Descriptive Writing*

Writing Situation: In this lesson you will write about the picture below.

Directions for Writing: Before you begin writing, you will use scratch paper to brainstorm and organize your ideas. It is important that you write clearly about the picture below and tell about all of the things you see. Use the notes you made on the scratch paper and stay organized.

Use the best English you can, but do not worry about mistakes. The most important thing is to describe the picture in interesting, colorful words.

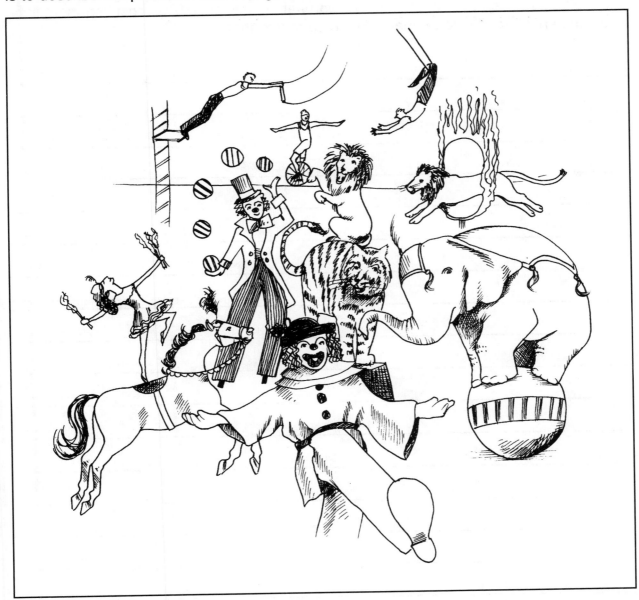

Name: _____ Date: _____

Student Writing Sample With Teacher Prompt— *Friendly Letter*

Writing Situation: In this lesson you will write a friendly letter.

Write a letter to a friend who has moved away. Tell your friend what you have been doing since he or she moved.

Directions for Writing: Before you begin writing, you will use scratch paper or the space below to brainstorm and organize your ideas. Make sure your letter contains all of the parts of a friendly letter.

Use the best English you can, but do not worry about mistakes. The most important thing is to write an interesting letter that is in the correct format.

_____

_____

_____

_____

_____

_____

_____

_____

_____

_____

_____

_____

_____

_____

_____

Name: _____ Date: _____

Student Writing Sample With Teacher Prompt—
Persuasive Essay

Writing Situation: In this lesson you will write a persuasive essay on one of the following topics:

- Year-round school
- School uniforms
- TV: Good or bad?

It is important to try to convince your readers to agree with you.

Directions for Writing: Before you begin writing, decide on your position, and then use scratch paper or the space below to list reasons to support your position.

Use the best English you can, but do not worry about mistakes. The most important thing is to write clearly and explain why you think your readers should agree with you. Use the notes you made on the scratch paper to help you stay organized.

_____

_____

_____

_____

_____

_____

_____

_____

_____

_____

_____

_____

_____

_____

_____

Name: _____ Date: _____

Section III: Writing Skills Test

Directions: Read each sentence. Darken the circle next to the <u>best</u> answer.

1. Which of these would be a personal narrative topic?
   - ○ A. A fairy tale
   - ○ B. A description of an unusual character
   - ○ C. The worst homework experience of your life
   - ○ D. A report on tornadoes

2. Which of each pair of beginnings would "grab" the reader's attention?
   - ○ A. I remember riding the roller coaster when I got sick.   **OR**
   - ○ B. While riding The Wild Corkscrew for the third time, I felt my stomach come into my throat.

   - ○ C. I visited The Haunted Mansion on Halloween.   **OR**
   - ○ D. "Eeeekkk," I yelled, as spider webs slid across my face.

   - ○ E. Crawling slowly up the wall was the biggest, hairiest spider I had ever seen. **OR**
   - ○ F. My greatest fear is a big hairy spider.

3. Which of these story beginnings is written in the <u>first person</u>?
   - ○ A. It was an average day in July.   **OR**
   - ○ B. I couldn't remember a hotter, more boring day in July.

   - ○ C. I saw the most unbelievable thing in town yesterday.   **OR**
   - ○ D. A boy in a pink ballet tutu walked by.

   - ○ E. Some people do not like sweets.   **OR**
   - ○ F. "Yuck," I cried, "you know I don't like sweets!"

4. Number these events in the order that makes sense.

   _____ A. I'm talking about a real haunted house, not some amusement park ride.

   _____ B. Once a bunch of my friends and I went to this old haunted house.

   _____ C. We couldn't go in at first because we were too scared.

   _____ D. We just kept talking about whether we should go in or not.

Name: _____ Date: _____

Section III: Writing Skills Test (cont.)

5. Number these events in the order that makes sense.

    _____ A. He had just been to a Yankees game.

    _____ B. Of course I knew.

    _____ C. I remember the day I got my prized possession.

    _____ D. He asked me if I knew who Mickey Mantle was.

    _____ E. The doorbell rang, and it was my dad's friend Tom.

    _____ F. Then he handed me a signed Mickey Mantle baseball.

    _____ G. He was one of the greatest ballplayers of all time.

6. Read the sentences below. All but <u>one</u> provide supporting details for the personal narrative prompt. Darken the circle of the choice that does <u>not</u> support the prompt.

    A. Mrs. Grundy is my neighbor.
        ○ 1. She lives in the pink house behind our house.
        ○ 2. She has a mean dog.
        ○ 3. Whenever my ball goes over her fence, her dog grabs it.
        ○ 4. Mrs. Grundy was robbed.
        ○ 5. If I ask her politely, she'll give my ball back.

    B. Our school was suddenly closed down.
        ○ 1. School officials gave no reason for it except to say it was necessary.
        ○ 2. The school is in the south part of town.
        ○ 3. All students were sent home.
        ○ 4. Parents and students guessed that the water was contaminated.
        ○ 5. There was no school today.

    C. Don't ever talk back to your mother.
        ○ 1. My dad was fixing the car.
        ○ 2. Boy, did I ever get in trouble!
        ○ 3. I said, "You aren't the boss of me."
        ○ 4. She grounded me for a week.
        ○ 5. It doesn't pay to stick up for yourself with your mother.

Name: _____ Date: _____

Section III: Writing Skills Test (cont.)

7. Which one of these sentences best shows the author's voice?
   - ○ A. The peppers in my salad were hot and spicy.
   - ○ B. The spicy peppers in my salad bit my tongue.
   - ○ C. Pepper juice was hot on my tongue.

8. Which one of these sentences best shows the author's voice?
   - ○ A. Our town was struck by a tornado.
   - ○ B. The houses were destroyed by the tornado.
   - ○ C. A thunderous tornado devastated our town last night.

9. Cross out any unneeded or repetitive ideas in each of the following sentences.

   A. I can't believe she totally ate the whole thing.

   B. The neatest gift I ever got was the bike I got for my birthday. It was my birthday, and I was having a party.

   C. In my opinion, I think the neighbor's swimming pool is a health hazard!

10. Rewrite each of these sentence to make the meaning clear.

    A. I got many old purses from my grandmother in beautiful condition.

    _____

    _____

    _____

    B. Stuck between the back of the sofa and the wall I found my overdue library book.

    _____

    _____

    _____

    C. My mom is selling a mixing bowl sure to please any cook with a round bottom.

    _____

    _____

    _____

Name: _____ Date: _____

Section III: Writing Skills Test (cont.)

11. Write a more colorful word above each underlined word or words.

    A. The elephant <u>walked</u> along behind the ringmaster.

    B. The parade <u>went on</u> for four hours.

    C. Did you <u>have</u> peanuts or cotton candy?

    D. Someone was <u>hiding</u> behind the clowns.

    E. The lights threw a <u>nice</u> yellow glow across the crowd.

12. Replace each underlined, ordinary word with a more colorful or interesting word. Write the new word above the underlined word.

    > I <u>got</u> this funny e-mail from my friend Ray. He <u>was</u>
    >
    > <u>going</u> to move away, and I <u>was feeling</u> <u>sad</u>. We always
    >
    > played <u>games</u> and <u>stuff</u> together. Where was he <u>going</u>?
    >
    > Who would be my <u>friend</u> now? I was <u>sad</u>.

13. Darken the circle next to the most satisfying ending for each of these writing prompts.

    A. A person to avoid
       ○ 1. I learned my lesson the hard way.
       ○ 2. I hope I never see him again. The End.
       ○ 3. He is certainly a person to avoid.

    B. The best gift
       ○ 1. My family is the best gift I ever received.
       ○ 2. What would I do without my sisters?
       ○ 3. I like my Teddy bear the best.

    C. A wild thunderstorm
       ○ 1. I'll never be alone in a thunderstorm again.
       ○ 2. This was the worst storm I ever experienced.
       ○ 3. And that's the end—of my story, and the storm.

Name: _____ Date: _____

Section III: Writing Skills Test (cont.)

14. Write a clear, interesting, complete sentence about one of these topics.

- A time when you felt worried
- Something you've seen that was enormous
- Something that always makes you laugh
- A troublesome mix-up
- A time you felt safe
- Your least-favorite dinner

_____

_____

_____

_____

15. Write a strong "grabber" beginning for one of these topics.

- A mysterious disappearance
- A visit with your dentist
- A favorite family memory
- A place you don't like to visit

_____

_____

_____

_____

16. Write a strong, satisfying ending for one of these topics.

- The worst Saturday you have ever experienced
- The best gift you have ever received
- Your favorite place to visit
- The chore you least like to do

_____

_____

_____

_____

Name: _____ Date: _____

Section III: Writing Skills Test (cont.)

17. Correct the grammar, spelling, and punctuation in the following personal narrative. Also eliminate unnecessary words or phrases. Use editor's marks to indicate corrections.

I got this e-mail and it was the best e-mail I ever got in it was from my friend joanna and she moved and i started crieying and the next thing somebody was knocking on the door and it was her and we played in the summer and she came in the right time and it was my birhathday and what I whanted to do let her pick where she whanted to go and she said kings iland and i said I whanted to go there two

18. Now rewrite this story so that it meets the criteria for a good personal narrative.

_____

_____

_____

_____

_____

_____

_____

_____

_____

_____

_____

Answer Keys

Unit 1: Writing a Friendly Letter (p. 3)

Heading:	21825 Regency Rd. Zap, ND 58580 February 8, 2001
Greeting:	Dear Kayte,
Body:	The text of the letter
Closing:	Your friend,
Signature:	Julia (handwritten)

Unit 1: Writing a Business Letter (p. 4)

Heading:	20110 Grandview Riverside, GA 12345
Date:	June 25, 2001
Inside Address:	Mr. Bart Smith Video Viewer 707 Salem Ave. Scottville, IL 62683
Greeting:	Dear Mr. Smith: (colon)
Body:	The text of the letter
Closing:	Sincerely,
Signature:	Lateesha Brown (handwritten and typed)

Unit 1: Writing a Narrative (p. 5)

Topic: A funny experience

Main Idea: A pig got loose and chased my mother.

Topic Sentence: The pig started chasing her around the exhibits.

Details: she looked hilarious; pulling the stroller up the stairs

Closing Sentence: This was a state fair our family will never forget!

Unit 1: Writing a Personal Narrative (p. 6)

All boxes should be checked.

Unit 1: Writing a Reflection (p. 10)

1. It tells what the writer thinks and feels.
2. Topic: Dog died
   Main Idea: Writer felt sad when Bailey died
   Topic Sentence: One of the saddest days of my life was when …
   Details: puppy; 13 years old; waited for me; ran with me
   Closing Sentence: She was a good dog and a faithful friend.

Unit 1: Writing Skills Test (p. 11–14)

1. A
2. C
3. A
4. D
5. C
6. A
7. C
8. A
9. C
10. B
11. D
12–13. Use evaluation rubrics to assess writing.

Unit 2: Writing a Persuasive Essay (p. 15)

Any reasonable answer is acceptable. Evaluate using criteria for ideas and organization.

Unit 2: Writing an Editorial (p. 16)

Stated position must have a beginning, middle, and end.

Unit 2: Writing a Persuasive Letter (p. 17)

Check to see if the writer appealed to reason, character, or emotions.

Unit 2: Writing a Letter to the Editor (p. 18)

1. He says he has eaten almost 750 lunches; it shows he has experience with the topic.
2. Yes.
3. It would be appreciated by a lot of students, it would be more nutritious, and it would add variety.
4. By asking the administration to consider offering a salad bar; there is no closing.
5. Answers will vary.

Unit 2: Writing a Letter of Request (p. 19)
1. To have Freddie Prinze, Jr., meet her friend Joanna.
2. She tells about her friend.
3. Her friend's desire to meet him before she dies; Joanna is worried about it taking too long to fulfill the wish.
4. No, she should use a business letter format.
5. She tells him they will still be fans.

Unit 2: Writing an Advertisement (p. 20)
1. An arts and crafts fair
2. people of all ages; things you want and stuff you didn't know you needed
3–4. Answers will vary.

Unit 2: Writing Skills Test (p. 21–24)
1. A
2. C
3. B
4. A
5. D
6. C
7. A
8. D
9. B
10–11. Use evaluation rubrics to assess writing.

Unit 3: Writing a Description 1 (p. 27)
1. Possible answers include:
   b. short, petite, tiny
   c. crimson, cardinal, russet
   d. filthy, dirty, sloppy, grubby
2. Example: While babysitting the cute twins next door, I watched a late-night horror movie.

Unit 3: Writing a Message (p. 31)
1. To have his mom pick him up at Sam's house
2. Yes.
3. No.
4. Yes; Please pick me up at 5:00 p.m.
5. Answers will vary.

Unit 3: Writing an Informational Paragraph (p. 32)
1. The first woman in space
2. Sally Ride was the first American woman in space.
3. Teacher check.
4. Answers will vary.

Unit 3: Writing Skills Test (p. 37–39)
1. B
2. A
3. D
4. C
5. C
6. D
7. A
8. B
9. A
10. C
11. D
12. Use evaluation rubrics to assess writing.

Unit 4: Writing Skills Test (p. 56–59)
1. D
2. A
3. B
4. C
5. D
6. C
7. B
8. D
9. A
10. A
11. C
12–13. Use evaluation rubrics to assess writing.

Unit 5: Choosing the Proper Format for Writing (p. 60)
1. personal narrative
2. persuasive essay or letter
3. individual report or collaborative report
4. story or play
5. journal
6. friendly letter
7. explanation
8. letter of request
9. advertisement
10. description

Unit 5: Writing Skills Test (p. 63–65)
1. C
2. D
3. A
4. B
5. D
6. C
7. A

8. B
9. A
10. D
11. B
12. C
13. Use evaluation rubrics to assess writing.

Unit 6: Capitalizing Proper Nouns (p. 67–68)
1. Men's World Cup, Uruguay
2. Uncle, France
3. Wildcats, Tigers
4. Dad, Illinois State Fair
5. correct
6. English, Spanish
7. Canada
8. Mr. Williamson, Sycamore
9. *The Diary of a Young Girl*
10. correct

Paragraph:

On July 10, 1999, the United States women's soccer team defeated china to win the 1999 world cup. The game was held at the rose bowl in pasadena, california, in front of a crowd of 90,185 people. This was the largest crowd to ever attend a women's sporting event in the united states. The game ended in a 0–0 tie, so the game had to be decided by a shoot-out. China kicked first and made 4 of 5 penalty kicks. The U.S. team made their first four kicks. It was all up to brandi chastain. If she made her shot, the united states would bring home the championship. Brandi's high, hard kick sailed to the top of the net over the head of the goalie, winning the shoot-out by a score of 5–4. Her teammates and the crowd were thrilled!

The women's world cup has been held three times, in 1991, 1995, and 1999. The united states has won twice, in 1991 and 1999. The next tournament is scheduled for 2003. The people of the united states hope the team wins again.

Unit 6: Capitalizing Titles and Abbreviations (p. 70)
1. Dr. Smith delivered a baby girl named Marie to the Brown family on Oak Ave.
2. J. K. Rowling is the author of <u>Harry Potter and the Sorcerer's Stone</u>.
3. Mrs. Elena Moreno lives at 406 Chicago Dr.
4. Mr. Buffington read the poem "Casey at the Bat" to our class today.
5. I wonder why Cassandra and Mitchell didn't come to see our play, <u>A Christmas Carol</u>.

Unit 6: Capitalizing Days and Months (p. 71)
1. At Tuesday's meeting, Rev. Martin scheduled the church picnic for Memorial Day.

2. Señora Hernandez told us that Cinco de Mayo is celebrated on May 5 in Los Angeles.
3. On Wednesday afternoon, I had an appointment with Dr. Jones, our dentist.
4. Thanksgiving Day is celebrated on the fourth Thursday in November.
5. The last day of church camp this summer will be Friday, August 18.

Unit 6: Capitalizing Academic Subjects and Languages (p. 72)
1. French
2. Fridays
3. German, Thanksgiving Day
4. Mr. Yoko, Japanese
5. correct
6. Melissa, I, European
7. English
8. correct
9. Melba, Spanish
10. I'm

Unit 6: Capitalizing Quotations (p. 73)
1. Senator John Dankin, a leading figure in the Republican Party, said, "We will win!"
2. "History will come alive," said Miss Thomas, our Asian history teacher.
3. correct
4. "How many students are in your class this year?" asked Jamie.
5. "Zack is the best batter on his team," I said, "and he's also a good pitcher."

Unit 6: Capitalizing Directions (p. 74)
1. correct
2. South Boston
3. West, L.A.
4. South Florida
5. Ms. Watson, North School
6. Civil War, North, South
7. South Service Station
8. Dr. Burton, West
9. East
10. West

Unit 6: Capitalization Test (p. 75–76)

1. C
2. B
3. A
4. C
5. B
6. A
7. C
8. D
9. A
10. A
11. A
12. B
13. B
14. B
15. C

Unit 7: Punctuation: Sentences (p. 77)

1. !
2. .
3. ?
4. ?
5. .
6. .
7. !
8. ?
9. ?
10. . or !
11. .
12. .
13. ?
14. .
15. !

Unit 7: Punctuation: The Period (p. 78)

1. My brother said, "I work for Dr. Who at the FBI."
2. Gen. Robert E. Lee led the Confederate Army during the Civil War.
3. My little sister watches Sesame St. almost every day during the summer.
4. The sign on Marwood Ave. said, "Stay Out."
5. The pilot, Bobby L. Lewis, makes traffic reports on station WZZK.

Unit 7: Punctuation: The Comma (p. 79)

President for a Day

Lana, the president of the student council, was absent from school, so I had to fill in for her. I had to call the meeting, make the announcements, record the minutes, and conduct the business. Many students were fooling around. "Let's get down to business," I said. Paul asked if I had heard the rumors about the new lunch program. I told him "Yes, I had heard the news." After much discussion, we decided to meet again on Monday, November 5, 2001. With all my duties as temporary president, I was tired and very glad the meeting was over!

Unit 7: Punctuation: Quotation Marks (p. 80)

1. Janet said, "I am going to the Philippine Islands on October 11, 2001."
2. "What are you going to do there?" asked Ruby Jewell.
3. "Well," she said, "I am going to work, play, and shop."
4. "Do people in the Philippine Islands speak English?" Thomas asked.
5. "Some do, some don't," Janet replied.

Unit 7: Punctuation: The Apostrophe (p. 81)

The Circus

The circus came to Yeats School last week. Yeats' circus was the greatest show on Earth. The clowns' tricks kept everyone laughing, especially when one clown's flower squirted water on the principal. The crowd's applause was loudest for the elephants' dance and the acrobats' skill. The boys' cheers were the loudest for the lion tamers' courage, but the lion's fierce roar scared them. The ringmasters' jokes were a big hit, and the performers' costumes were admired by all. Yeats' circus was a great success!

Unit 7: Punctuation Test (p. 82–83)

1. D
2. B
3. C
4. A
5. D
6. B
7. C
8. C
9. B
10. D
11. C
12. C

13. B
14. D
15. A

Unit 8: Usage: Sentence Fragments (p. 84)
1. fragment
2. fragment
3. sentence
4. fragment
5. sentence
6. sentence
7. fragment
8. sentence
9. sentence
10. fragment
11. sentence
12. fragment
13. sentence
14. fragment
15. fragment

Unit 8: Usage: Run-on Sentences (p. 85)
1. George Washington was commander in chief of the Continental Army. He was a great horseman.
2. George Washington married Martha Custis. She was a widow with two children.
3. While a young man, he spent a lot of time outdoors. He also enjoyed dancing.
4. The White House did not exist while Washington was president. John Adams was the first president to live there.
5. George Washington inherited the plantation, Mount Vernon. It is located in Virginia.
6. He created a medal to recognize merit in the military. It was called the Purple Heart.
7. While her husband was president, Martha's formal title was not Mrs. Washington. She was addressed as Lady Washington.
8. There are many myths about Washington. Many of these were written about in two books by Parson Mason Weems.
9. One of the most popular myths was about George chopping down a cherry tree. He confessed to his father.
10. Washington served eight years as president. He retired to Mount Vernon.

Unit 8: Usage: Simple and Compound Sentences (p. 86)
Answers may vary. Possible answers include:
1. The workers at the school were told to put their oily rags in cans, but they forgot to do it.
2. During the night, the rags caught fire, and the fire spread quickly through the storeroom.
3. The smoke detector blared loudly, but no one heard it.
4. A neighbor called 911 because she saw flames shooting out of the windows.
5. Firefighters raced to the school and saw smoke pouring out of a hole in the roof.
6. Glass cracked from the heat of the fire and shattered all over the sidewalk.
7. The firefighters needed more help, so the captain called in another company.
8. Finally, after almost four hours, the fire was brought under control.
9. Luckily, school was closed for summer vacation, so no one was there at the time.
10. It's going to take about a month to clean and fix up the building because it is a real mess.

Unit 8: Usage: Precise Words (p. 87)
1. dog, roses/poppies
2. angry, damage/destruction, garden
3. embarrassed, destruction/damage
4. apologize, vibrant, poppies/roses
5. grinned, canine
6. sensible, confine
7. escape, mischief
8. obedient, sometimes
9. teach, behave
10. enjoys, repair

Unit 8: Usage: Verbs That Agree (p. 88)
1. was
2. are
3. were
4. is
5. are
6. does
7. desire
8. wants
9. is, is
10. comes, sees, prevent

Unit 8: Usage: "How Many?" Adjectives (p. 89)

1. fewer
2. more, less
3. fewer
4. number
5. Less
6. number
7. much
8. number
9. many
10. fewer
11. more
12. fewer
13. many
14. number, more
15. less

Unit 8: Usage: Pronouns and Their Homophones (p. 90)

Poison Frogs

Everyone has seen a frog. <u>Their</u> [They're] a familiar sight around marshes and ponds. <u>Their</u> [There] is another kind of frog, however, that is very poisonous. Only a tiny pinprick of <u>it's</u> [its] skin secretion is enough to kill a human being. If <u>your</u> [you're] in South or Central America, look out for this black and yellow frog. <u>Its</u> [It's] the kind of frog you don't want in <u>you're</u> [your] suitcase.

1. their
2. your, it's
3. there
4. They're
5. its

Unit 8: "Good" Adjectives and "Well" Adverbs (p. 91)

1. good
2. well
3. well
4. well
5. good
6. well
7. well
8. good
9. good
10. good
11. well
12. good
13. good
14. well
15. good

Unit 8: Usage Test (p. 92–93)

1. A
2. B
3. C
4. C
5. B
6. B
7. B
8. B
9. A
10. B
11. A
12. A
13. B
14. A
15. B

Section III: Writing Skills Test (p. 114–119)

1. C
2. B
   D
   E
3. B
   C
   F
4A. 2
B. 1
C. 3
D. 4
5A. 3
B. 5
C. 1
D. 4
E. 2
F. 7
G. 6
6A. 4
B. 2
C. 1
7. B
8. C
9A. Cross out: totally
B. Cross out: It was my birthday, and I was having a party.
C. Cross out: In my opinion,

10–12. Answers will vary. Possible answers include:

10A. I got many old purses in beautiful condition from my grandmother.

  B. I found my overdue library book stuck between the back of the sofa and the wall.

  C. My mom is selling a mixing bowl with a round bottom sure to please any cook.

11. Answers will vary. Possible answers include:

  A. lumbered

  B. wound on

  C. consume

  D. lurking

  E. gentle

12. Answers will vary. Possible answers include:

  I received this funny e-mail from my friend Ray. He planned to move away, and I became devastated. We always played kickball and checkers together. Where was he moving? Who would be my compadre now? I was blue.

13A. 1

  B. 2

  C. 3

14–16. Accept any reasonable answers.

17.   Paragraph:

18.   Use evaluation rubrics to assess writing.